Evaluating
Teachers
for
Professional
Growth

Evaluating Teachers for Professional Growth

Daniel R. Beerens

Creating a Culture of Motivation and Learning

CORWIN PRESS, INC.
A Sage Publications Company
Thousand Oaks, California

For information:

Corwin Press, Inc.
A Sage Publications Company
2455 Teller Road
Thousand Oaks, California 91320
E-mail: order@corwinpress.com

Sage Publications Ltd.
6 Bonhill Street
London EC2A 4PU
United Kingdom

Sage Publications India Pvt. Ltd.
M-32 Market
Greater Kailash I
New Delhi 110 048 India

Printed in the United States of America

Library of Congress Cataloging-in-Publication Data

Beerens, Daniel R.
    Evaluating teachers for professional growth: Creating a
culture of motivation and learning / by Daniel R. Beerens.
        p.   cm.
    Includes bibliographical references and index.
    ISBN 0-7619-7566-7 (cloth)
    ISBN 0-7619-7567-5 (pbk.)
    1. Teachers—Rating of—United States.   2. Teacher
effectiveness—United States.   I. Title.
    LB2838 .B44 2000
    371.14′4′0973—dc21   99-6723

This book is printed on acid-free paper.

00   01   02   03   04   05   06   7   6   5   4   3   2

Corwin Editorial Assistant: Kylee Liegl
Production Editor: Denise Santoyo
Editorial Assistant: Cindy Bear
Typesetter/Designer: Lynn Miyata
Cover Designer: Oscar Desierto

Contents

PART II

Preface

The role of the principal is crucial in establishing a culture for learning. Combining the best thinking from the worlds of education and business, this book describes effective ways for principals and teachers to work together for the teachers' growth and the ultimate benefit of students' learning. It provides a solid philosophical foundation for significant change in teacher evaluation and staff development. Past methods and current trends in the field are analyzed.

Is there a practical approach that incorporates the best practice in management theory, emotional intelligence, and educational research into a usable package? This book spells out a field-tested system that addresses the need of the principal to serve in the roles of evaluator, staff developer, instructional leader, and collaborative coach. The reader can immediately implement this system by using the reproducible forms found in Resource A.

Evaluating Teachers for Professional Growth: Creating a Culture of Motivation and Learning is a wonderful addition to the available body of professional discussion on the topic. It presents a clear, logical, and readable road map for positive and meaningful change in teacher evaluation; the rest is up to the reader!

Acknowledgments

I express my appreciation to the following people:

- My wife, Sheryl, who has always believed in me and encouraged me. Only my love for her surpasses my respect for her intelligence, educational professionalism, and wisdom. I could not have done this work without her constant support, editorial assistance, and love.

- My daughters, Stephanie and Julie, who are bright beams of joy in my life and who understandingly gave up seeing their dad while this work was being completed.

■ My professional colleague and friend Bart DenBoer, who shared a similar discontent with the status quo and was willing to take some risks along with me. Our many conversations on this topic and our joint efforts for change have been professionally expanding and satisfying.

■ My superintendent, Glenn Vos, for believing in the merit of this system, for supporting the implementation of the system, and for helpful suggestions after his review of the draft manuscript.

■ Charlotte Danielson for her support of this project, as well as for permission to use parts of her *Framework for Teaching* within this book.

■ Joan St. Clair and Dave Neifer at the Ottawa Intermediate School District, who encouraged and supported the development of this system at crucial stages.

■ My editor at Corwin Press, Robb Clouse, for his assistance and encouragement on this project, and also his assistant, Kylee Liegl, for her help.

■ The reviewers who helped shape the manuscript: Dr. Jody Dunlap, Assistant Superintendent, Personnel Services, Conejo Valley Unified School District, Thousand Oaks, California; G. Steven Griggs, Associate Principal, Francis Howell Central High School, St. Charles, Missouri; Dr. Larry Leapley, Director of Curriculum, Trenton Public Schools, Trenton, Michigan; Dr. Mary Beth Poole, Adjunct Graduate Professor, East Carolina University, Greenville, North Carolina; Barbara Ryan, Director of Elementary Education, Conejo Valley Unified School District, Thousand Oaks, California; and Dr. Susan Villani, Principal, Thoreau School, Concord, Massachusetts.

—Dan Beerens

About the Author

Daniel R. Beerens began his teaching career by working with children with behavior disorders in an urban public school setting. He also taught fourth-grade and middle school students with physical disabilities in suburban private and public school settings.

After receiving his master's degree in educational leadership at National-Louis University, he served as principal of several elementary and middle schools. Within each district, he was significantly involved in systemwide curricular change and program development. He has presented on teacher evaluation and professional growth at regional and national conferences.

He can be reached via e-mail: bbeerens@remc7.K12.mi.us

Introduction

Teacher evaluation and professional growth are among the most complex issues in education, as well as two of the most important. No one seems to have a complete answer to the best ways to meet the growth needs of the teacher and the supervisory needs of the administrator. The evaluation process can be frustrating for both teacher and administrator.

My interest in this topic has grown out of my own discontent with the status quo, a belief that there has to be a better way, and a conscientious desire to achieve a workable and possibly even a valuable solution for both parties involved. My quest for a workable solution has led me through years of sustained reading of the professional literature regarding staff evaluation and professional development and into the leadership literature of the business world. Coincidentally, during the past 15 years, significant changes have taken place in business and education in terms of understanding what effective leadership is, how people can be encouraged to grow and develop, and how management theory has shifted significantly to recognize the value of the person over the organization. These shifts are a major encouragement to me as I consider how we have improved both a people and a quality focus in what we do. I have often stated to friends that I do not think I would have entered the world of administration had the hierarchical style of management remained the dominant mode.

Teaching is a complex endeavor. Many intellectual, emotional, spiritual, and physical demands are placed on teachers as they seek appropriate resources, teaching methods, and assessment techniques to make learning meaningful for each student. The job is emotionally draining if done with intensity, passion, and love. Classroom environment and management, planning and preparation, instruction, and professional responsibilities are all essential components in student instruction. Development of the teacher as a professional is key to a successful learning culture within a school. It is my intent in this book to explore the past issues of evaluation and supervision, to look at the best current thinking about teacher motivation and growth, and then to suggest a practical and sound approach for staff evaluation and professional development.

In Chapter 1, I explore and share some questions I'm sure all principals ask as they face the responsibility of teacher evaluation and supervision. I believe that what administrators desire deep down is a system that reduces tension between teachers and administrators during the process yet is effective and provides accountability. Both teachers and administrators also want a program that leads to sustained and meaningful professional growth for the teachers. They would like to be able to believe that what they are doing not only meets the requirements of their job but, more important, also improves their school and the success of their students.

In Chapter 2, I explore the significance of the teacher and the complexity of the work of teaching. As administrators, why expend our energies in places other than working with our teachers if we really want to improve our schools? Increasingly, we are recognizing the complexity of teaching. We need to acknowledge that this complexity makes evaluation difficult and ineffective if we continue to use old models and systems. Why do the old models have limited effectiveness?

In Chapter 3, I discuss the purposes and types of evaluation, along with the limitations of the principal as evaluator. Principals have tried many methods over many years, and here I examine some recent approaches. What have been the weaknesses of these approaches? What are teacher and administrator concerns regarding the evaluation process?

Looking outside the world of education, we search through the leadership literature for valuable insights that may give us direction in working with and leading others. In Chapter 4, I deal with the person of the leader. How does he or she encourage and motivate others and in doing so create a culture of learning?

Next, I turn to the teacher and in Chapter 5 seek to understand what motivates teachers, the professional aspects of teaching, and the best ways adults learn. What are the linkages and relationships among evaluation, instruction, and staff development? How does the principal play a key role in these three areas?

In Chapter 6, I summarize the many factors that have encouraged educators to look at alternative means of evaluating teachers. Why do we need a new approach? Why should we encourage reflective practice and self-assessment with our teachers? What about portfolios, peer coaching and evaluation, 360-degree feedback? What are the positives and negatives of these new approaches? Does any approach give teachers freedom and options and also meet administrative needs?

In Chapter 7, I explain the approach that a colleague and I have developed to meet both evaluation and professional growth needs. It is called the *Growth-Focused Evaluation System.* Succeeding chapters are a practical articulation of this material: Chapter 8 deals with how to divide teachers into three types and to provide differentiated supervision with each group. Chapter 9 presents the teaching practice standards from the book *Enhancing Professional Practice: A Framework for Teaching* (Danielson, 1996), and I am deeply grateful to the author, Charlotte Danielson, for her permission to use the standards in this book. A key component of the system is using these standards to promote professional conversations, goal setting, and evaluation. Chapter 10 presents the structures, processes, and instruments we have developed to promote teacher reflection and examination of practice in the Growth-Focused Evaluation System. Processes for working with the experienced teacher, the beginning or transferring teacher, and the marginal teacher are explained, forms are included, and examples of teacher and administrator work are shared.

In Chapter 11, I provide sample summaries of how to report teacher growth and evaluation for other accountability purposes. I look at a sample system of professional growth in Chapter 12, as well as at ways teachers can record their professional growth and activity over a period of years. Finally, in Chapter 13 I encourage you to take action. Resource A, an appendix of forms at the end of the book, provides masters that can be reproduced as you develop your own plan or implement the plan described.

After having developed and used the Growth-Focused Evaluation System during the past several years, I have found it to be a practical system that embodies the latest research and best thinking on teaching, learning, leadership, and human development. It is based on the theories found in Chapters 2 through 6 of this book and my own personal experience as a teacher and administrator during the past 18 years. I do not view the Growth-Focused Evaluation System as a finished product because I believe that people's best work is always in the process of becoming. Growth and refinement must be a continuous process. I look forward to further learning and conversation on this topic and hope to continue to learn much from other practitioners. I hope you are able to take something from this book and make your own school reality more meaningful.

In summary, the Growth-Focused Evaluation System has several purposes:

- Seeks to articulate a process for sustained professional growth

- Describes the standards of professional practice

- Offers a variety of methods and strategies for growth and accountability

- Provides a record of professional growth over a period of years

■ Ultimately provides a tool for professional conversation so that, together, teachers and administrators may communicate about excellence for students

As Linda Darling-Hammond (1997) states:

Successful 21st-century schools will be grounded on two very different presumptions: first, that teaching matters and, second, that relationships matter . . . Principals are finding that the job of leading schools is increasingly one of creating structures and strategies that support skillful teaching and strengthen productive relationships. (p. 1)

It is my hope that this book will not only provide helpful background philosophy and theory but also be practical enough that you may begin to use the Growth-Focused Evaluation System structure, components, processes, instruments, and examples as they are or as models to spur you to develop your thinking further in the area of teacher evaluation and professional growth.

PART I

CHAPTER ONE

More Questions Than Answers

As a beginning administrator, fresh from graduate school and armed with clinical supervision and effective teaching behaviors training, I certainly approached the evaluation process with a certain amount of fear and trembling. Why should older and more experienced teachers listen to what I had to say about their teaching? Many had been teaching in their area of expertise for years, and it seemed presumptuous that I would have something truly worthwhile to add. How could I begin to understand the dynamic of their classroom or the particular student needs present in it? Wouldn't they just politely smile at any naive suggestions I would later make to them during the observation postconference? How did I know that my carefully crafted and diplomatically stated comments would make a real difference in their teaching practice? What was the point of it all, anyway? Did it really matter?

I expected these questions to disappear as I gained more experience and confidence as an administrator, but they remained unresolved dilemmas. Each year, the weeks around evaluation time became more distasteful as I realized that I had not resolved the problems I saw with teacher evaluations but once again had to make it through a meaningless process. How could I be credible with my teachers in making suggestions about their teaching? I felt more and more hypocritical as I pretended to be the all-knowing school instructional leader. I knew that there were never enough hours in the day to truly be an instructional leader in the ways I wanted to be. Even if I could turn myself into an expert in all areas and perfectly identify deficiencies, would my words and advice make any difference? How could I be sure that teachers would put into practice what I had suggested? How could I develop professionalism and ownership in my faculty?

As a principal in two highly regarded districts of suburban Chicago, I was required not only to provide narrative comments but also to rank teachers as unacceptable, average, excellent, or superior! New principals into the district faced the difficulty of inheriting a predecessor's subjective ratings. Some teachers made it clear to me that they had always received superior rankings and that they expected me to follow suit. I began to question whether any ranking other than superior motivated anyone. I got the impression that most of my teachers weren't really interested in my narrative comments until they knew the ranking I had given. I wondered whether some of those who consistently received a superior ranking were getting complacent. I debated the wisdom of reducing the inflated rating of some teachers to a more realistic average ranking. It seemed foolhardy, however, to stick my neck out by giving a lower ranking. I would not only face grief and anger from those teachers but also risk losing a working relationship with them. Compounding the problem was the fact that within the district the administrative team was not trained in how to evaluate, and consequently there was no reliability or consistency. Administrators received pressure from the school board to provide greater differentiation in the rankings of teachers. When teachers from various buildings talked to each other, they became disgruntled by the inequities of the rankings. Interestingly, in one large district where I worked, we did an internal study of administrator rankings and found that some buildings were loaded with "superior" teachers, whereas other buildings only had "average" teachers, with a few "excellent" thrown in! Given the quality of the teacher candidate pool and the culture of high standards for teaching performance, it was unlikely that the rankings were an accurate measure.

Throughout the majority of the year, it seemed that I could have a normal relationship with teachers and engage in appropriate coaching and encouragement activities. When evaluation time rolled around, however, an uneasy tension became palpable and the anxiety level for both my teachers and myself escalated. Even after a relaxed preconference chat and observation of a successful teaching lesson, I would sense that teachers would grow increasingly anxious until the very end of the postconference; they kept waiting for "the shoe to drop." I certainly thought I was low-key and reassuring, but they were nervous and defensive. How could I remove this fear so that we could have a meaningful professional conversation and make real progress together?

The more I read about leadership, the more my discontent with the conflicts between what I read concerning how to develop and bring out the best out in people and what we were practicing in educational administration grew. Dissonance existed between my personal values and the values of the typical evaluation process. I was not able to respond to teachers as I wanted, and I knew that I was putting them through a meaningless and anxiety-producing ritual each year. As the instructional leader, I wanted to be connected to the development of each of my teachers, but in the role of supervisor and evaluator I could not gain the trust of the teachers to my satisfaction so that meaningful development could occur. Was I helping them develop as professionals and take charge of their own learning?

What would happen if teachers had other choices besides the administrative evaluation? Would they be enabled to learn from each other? I was moving into participatory management practices as a principal, so why couldn't teachers participate in their own evaluations? Did the evaluation have to remain a process that was *done* to them? How could I let them participate and still carry out the responsibilities charged to me as an administrator? I could not rest until I either discovered or developed a system that allowed me to feel good about how I was working with people and at the same time getting tangible results related to student achievement. I had to find lasting principles and philosophical harmony—a system of evaluation and professional growth that I could believe in wholeheartedly. The following chapters unfold the kinds of issues I wrestled with and considered as I sought a solution to my dilemma.

CHAPTER TWO

The Significance of Teachers and the Complexity of Their Work

Starting With the Most Important Aspect—The Teacher

The teacher is the indispensable element in the school. In the report *What Matters Most: Teaching for America's Future*, the National Commission on Teaching and America's Future asserts that

> teacher expertise is the single most important determinant of student achievement. Recent studies consistently show that each dollar spent on recruiting high-quality teachers, and deepening their knowledge and skills, nets greater gains in student learning than any other use of an education dollar. (Ferguson, Greenwald, Hedges, & Laine as cited in Darling-Hammond, 1997, p. 1)

As administrators, we tend to spend lots of time and energy on other, peripheral issues when instead we should be working in the area of teacher growth and development. Education reformers over the past 12 years have reminded us that, to improve student achievement, we must improve teacher performance and quality.

As a result of his longitudinal study on student achievement, researcher William Sanders (1998), from the University of Tennessee at Knoxville, states: "What we have consistently found in this research, starting back in the early 1980s, is that the single largest factor affecting academic growth among students is the teacher. The teacher effects make all other effects pale in comparison" (p. 3). Sanders found that students in some teachers' classes consistently showed more improvement than students in other teachers' classes and that the effects were still evident 3 or 4 years later. He states that differences in teachers can account for differences in test scores of as much as 50 or 60 percentile points (as cited in Jones, 1997). Studies conducted in the Dallas school district yielded similar results (Archer, 1998a). In Boston, 10th-grade students who had started with similar baseline scores showed that the best teachers produced six times as much growth as the least effective teachers (Sava, 1998).

These results certainly direct our attention to the significance of the person of the teacher and encourage us as administrators to make the effectiveness of our teachers a top priority.

The Complexity of Teaching

As we learn more about brain research and how the mind works, we begin to gain a greater appreciation for the complexity of the human mind and the act of teaching. When we multiply the individual complexity times the number of students in a classroom, it becomes an amazing task to ask one person to keep the attention of all those minds and guide each down a path of meaningful learning.

Each moment of teaching is uncertain because of the possible response of anyone inside or outside the room. The teacher is continually receiving information from the students, whether speaking or listening, and is making split-second decisions about whether to continue, stop, or redirect the instruction. The teacher is often isolated and forced to be self-reliant at crucial moments of decision making. Teachers must continually and consciously weigh the impact of their words or actions, make decisions without reflection or deliberation, and adjust methods or expectations for different students. Research tells us that teachers make 3,000 nontrivial decisions daily (Danielson, 1996). The physical, intellectual, and emotional demands of teaching are very significant.

In calling teaching "one of the most complex human endeavors imaginable," Saphier and Gower (1997) point out that the good teacher is both a caring person and a skillful practitioner. McGreal (1993) defines good teaching as knowledge of content in a specific area, knowing how to teach that particular content, general teaching knowledge, and knowledge of the students. Of course, knowledge of the students includes knowing how to motivate them appropriately. After surveying 1,200 teachers, Shedd (as cited in Airasian, 1995) concluded that teaching is fundamentally a decision-making process requiring the teacher to exercise discretion and judgment in situations that do not allow the application of predefined solutions to clearly delineated problems.

In their excellent review of the literature, Airasian and Gullickson (1997) cite four characteristics of teachers' classroom lives:

1. *Uncertainty.* Often lacking are (a) clear guidelines for decision making and (b) ways to measure the effectiveness of decisions that have been made.

2. *Complexity.* Many dimensions, situational contingencies, and sets of skills are operating at the same time.

3. *Practicality.* Teachers form practical solutions to their specific situations on the basis of common sense, experience, and thoughtful speculation, rather than on theory or course-specific knowledge.

4. *Individuality.* Teachers rely on their own values, beliefs, and intuition about teaching and learning.

Lee Shulman (as quoted in Perkins, 1992) summarizes:

Teaching is impossible. If we simply add together all that is expected of a typical teacher and take note of the circumstances under which those activities are to be carried out, the sum makes greater demands than any individual can possibly fulfill. Yet, teachers teach. (p. 51)

Any newly designed system of evaluation must account for the growing recognition of the complexity of teaching. It must develop the skill, intuition, and judgment of teachers and be meaningful for the context in which they function.

CHAPTER THREE

Approaches to Evaluation

Why evaluate teachers? What approaches have been tried? Which have proved successful, and which have been abandoned? What limitations do principals face in the evaluation process?

I believe that there are three main reasons to evaluate teachers:

1. To improve teacher effectiveness
2. To encourage professional growth
3. To remediate or eliminate weak teachers

Two reasons stated above deal with the development of teachers; one relates to making a judgment about the competence of a teacher for reasons of future assistance or employment.

My assumption, based on research, is that faculty growth and development must occur if we are to increase student achievement. The bottom line on the purpose of evaluating teachers must remain related to increasing student achievement. As we will see later, I attempt to make a case for teacher evaluation being the key to staff development and any meaningful school improvement. I argue that it is the most important activity in which a principal can engage within his or her school.

One problem with teacher evaluation is that it has been used for two purposes: (a) helping the teacher improve (formative evaluation) and at the same time (b) determining the future employment status of the teacher (summative). The principal is usually the person asked to carry out both functions: coaching, encouraging, developing, and assisting the teacher throughout the year and then at the end of the year making a summative judgment about the competence of the teacher. Stanley and Popham (1988) aver: "Even though many principals believe that they can, via trust-inducing behavior, be both the helper-person and the hatchet-person, such beliefs are mistaken" (p. 59). Robert Garmston describes the difficulty of this relationship by suggesting that the principal must be careful to avoid appearing to be "a barking dog whose tail is wagging" (as cited in O'Neil, 1993). Having one person responsible for both formative and summative aspects results in conflicts of interest and a lack of trust between teacher and administrator.

Past practices in supervision and evaluation suffer from serious deficiencies. For many years, the hierarchical "factory" model of check and inspect has been the dominant mode of teacher evaluation. Acheson and Gall (1987) credit this development historically to early 18th-century "inspectors" whose job was later assumed by a "principal" teacher at each school. They report that, despite many other models having been advocated over the years, many principals still view their supervisory role as that of inspector.

Two cartoons illustrate well the problems with this model from an administrator's and a classroom teacher's perspective. In the first cartoon, the nonplussed administrator stands and watches as teachers dance on the stage under the title "Teacher Performance Appraisal." Certainly, teachers can put on a good show with a tried-and-true "sure winner" lecture or teaching activity for the benefit of the administrator doing the observation. How many times a week would a teacher's classroom need to be observed to get a true picture? Probably many more times than the administrator could fit into the schedule. The second cartoon shows a startled teacher looking wide-eyed at a principal who says, "Your evaluation is based on what you do in the next 30 seconds. Go!" Obviously, this tactic is not fair to the teacher, but from a principal's viewpoint, that is sometimes about how much time one supposes is available, given all the other responsibilities of the job. To make matters worse for administrators who have been conscientious, Schmoker (as quoted in Marshall, 1996) tells us that "conventional evaluation, the kind the overwhelming majority of American teachers undergo, does not have any measurable impact on the quality of student learning. In most cases, it's a waste of time" (p. 336).

Traditional evaluation methods using rating scales have been shown to have several problems: They are high inference and very subjective in nature, lack reliability over time, are demotivational (as discussed earlier, everyone wants to be superior), and are subject to the halo effect—the overall impression a teacher makes on the rater. Medley, Coker, and Soar (1984) found that rating scales "reflect the beliefs of the rater about the nature of competent teacher performance rather than the actual competence of the performance" (p. 48). In the work of quality guru W. Edwards Deming, the de-emphasis of grading, rating, and ranking is fundamental to the success of his approach. Holt (1993) states,

> These (ranking and rating) are all ways in which we make judgements about people not in terms of who they are and the context in which they think or act, but in terms of their measured performance in response to some specified task. How can we believe that performance can be separated from the circumstances—the systems, to use Deming's term, that give rise to it. (p. 329)

William Glasser, in *The Quality School Teacher* (1993), based on the work of Deming, emphasizes that all our motivation comes from within and that "boss-managers" misunderstand this and attempt to motivate from the outside. Similarly, Lezotte, in *Creating the Total Quality Effective School* (1993), also based on Deming's TQM work and the effective schools movement, recommends in Principle 12: "Remove barriers that rob people of pride and workmanship. Eliminate the annual rating or merit system." His corresponding Effective Schools Tenets are as follows: "Teacher evaluation should include teacher self-evaluation, peer observations, and peer coaching. Teachers must be freed from the fear of negative evaluation if they are going to engage willingly in a process to improve the quality of their professional work" (p. 3). According to McGreal, "No single idea or concept has been more detrimental to successful teacher evaluation than the rating scale" (as cited in Stanley & Popham, 1988, p. 24).

Darling-Hammond and Sclan (1992), in the Association for Supervision and Curriculum Development (ASCD) *Supervision in Transition*, discuss the trend of the last 20 years: the behavioral approach that seeks to identify effective teaching behaviors from correlational research. This type of evaluation strategy has been criticized for failing to encourage or assess teacher effectiveness and for focusing only on displays of behaviors rather than identifying and solving actual problems of practice. The necessary observation and tally of specific teacher behaviors does not allow judgment for the appropriateness or effectiveness of the behaviors. Teaching behaviors found to be effective in some situations are ineffective or even counterproductive when used too much or under the wrong circumstances. Principals find the actual process of tallying by using the instruments suggested in this approach to be cumbersome and difficult to execute. Furthermore, students' performances on tasks requiring higher order skills, creativity, and problem-solving abilities benefit from very different instructional approaches than this teaching approach.

Other researchers have found that effective teaching behaviors vary, depending on student characteristics, subject matter demands, and instructional goals (Costa & Garmston, 1985). A major problem with inferring generalized rules for practice from correlational studies is that cause-effect relationships are unproved. In other words, teachers need to be able to vary their behavior across teaching situations to be effective—the art of teaching. The focus on the teaching behaviors approach to evaluation frequently reduces rather than enhances a teacher's effectiveness. It is interesting to note that Florida's 1986 Teacher of the Year did not pass the Florida Performance Measurement System Assessment when being evaluated for merit pay! Lawsuits and the overall limitations of systems that seek to use context-free behavioral indicators as the primary basis for evaluation have led many states to abandon this type of approach.

Clinical supervision of teachers was advanced in recent years as the best answer to the supervision riddle. It was a significant step forward in that it "is interactive rather than directive, democratic rather than authoritarian, teacher-centered rather than supervisor-centered" (Acheson & Gall, 1987, pp. 10-11). Through a preconference with the teacher, the administrator seeks to understand better the context of the situation and the teaching activity slated to occur. Although clinical supervision is still a useful tool for the purpose of working with the beginning or transferring teacher, it has not proved helpful to most teachers. Glatthorn and Coble (1995) believe that clinical supervision should be abandoned because "two or three perfunctory evaluations followed by 'good news/bad news' conferences are a waste of everyone's time" (p. 35).

Let's now explore in greater detail teacher and principal concerns about the use of clinical supervision. Experienced teachers do not believe that evaluations are productive. Boyd (1989) lists several reasons: (a) Teachers do not have input into evaluation criteria and therefore distrust the process and question the validity of the results the process produces; (b) evaluators do not spend enough time on the evaluation because principals are too busy to gather quality information and provide useful feedback; (c) evaluations are done on a sporadic basis; (d) evaluators are not well trained and have little classroom experience, and evaluations are vague, subjective, and inconsistent, leading to a lack of evaluator credibility; and (e) the evaluation process is a dead end as few districts have established a clear link between teacher evaluation and teacher development. Research conducted by Wiles, Cogan, and Blumberg (as cited in Acheson & Gall, 1987) shows that only a small fraction of teachers view their supervisors as a source of new ideas, that supervision is almost always viewed as a threat by the teacher and a source of undermining teacher confidence, and that teachers view supervision as a ritual no longer relevant. Teachers dismiss the annual observation as superficial, undiagnostic, unnecessary, and based on factors that have little relationship to instruction (Shedd; Kottkamp, Provenzo, & Cohn; Duke & Stiggins, as cited in Airasian, 1995). They do not see it as a tool for improving their practice. Teacher hostility to supervision is evident from the research. Teachers view evaluation as something done to them, initiated by someone else whose opinions they may or may not respect.

From the principal's point of view, past models of supervision also have many difficulties. As I mentioned earlier, one chief difficulty is a lack of time to evaluate. How much time would be adequate to evaluate a situation with integrity? How many evaluations is the typical principal responsible for in the course of a year? Principals probably have not received extensive training in evaluation. They may have had a course or two in a master's program in administration, and their university professors may have been predisposed to a certain viewpoint on the subject rather than taken a broad look at various methods. Furthermore, how can the principal be an expert in a wide range of disciplines and corresponding specialized instructional strategies? Shulman (as cited in O'Neil, 1993) questions the extent to which a "generalist" administrator can help teachers improve their teaching of specific subjects.

When principals are placed in an evaluative role, they often focus on superficial issues because the teacher denies them access to the real issues and dilemmas he or she faces daily (Blumberg & Jonas, as cited in Nolan & Francis, 1992). This predicament can be very discouraging for the principal because it demonstrates a lack of trust in the relationship and because there is little hope for having significant conversations with the teacher that will lead to meaningful instructional improvement. Lack of interpersonal skills by the principal can also lead to a lack of trust and respect by the teacher in the evaluation process. Because of their lack of comfort and confidence, administrators sometimes neglect to do anything about evaluation and supervision of teachers at all.

Concurrently as administrators have labored under the belief that they must be the instructional leaders and "have a handle on everything," the demands of school life, the information explosion, and the rate of change have shattered the illusion that, indeed, one superhuman individual can do it all. Hoerr (1996) states:

> It is simply not realistic to expect an administrator to serve as an intellectual resource or catalyst for all these (varied curriculum, child development, philosophical, and teaching and learning issues) efforts . . . the role of the principal has become increasingly complex as society has made ever-greater demands on the schools. (p. 380)

Principals with integrity and the courage to be honest with themselves realize that they are not the source of all knowledge. They know that they are not superhuman, and they are tired of pretending that all the answers reside in themselves. Because of current practice in the field or perhaps because of the pressure of school boards or the public for accountability, principals have felt forced to subscribe to and carry out practices that do not reflect their own values and beliefs. It is time for a change.

CHAPTER FOUR

Leadership, Growth, and Community

The person of the leader is critical to the success of any enterprise. Recent leadership literature has pointed out the significance of the leader's personal and moral values to the success of the organization. Studies reveal that emotional intelligence is much more essential for leaders than high intelligence as measured in traditional ways. What important aspects of leadership have recent authors confirmed to be true from both experience and research? What are the most effective and enduring ways to demonstrate leadership in order to help people achieve their potential? How do effective leaders build communities of learning and empowerment? Any evaluation and professional growth system must incorporate the best principles of leadership if it is to have a long-term chance of success. Two widely recognized writers—Stephen Covey (1991) from the world of business and Thomas Sergiovanni (1992) from the field of education—list similar sources of management authority or management paradigms. These are reflected in Table 4.1 and are helpful to our understanding of the different paradigms of management.

As we move down Table 4.1, we begin to understand the limitations of emphasizing only one aspect of human nature to the exclusion of others. The principle-centered/moral authority paradigm shown in the bottom row emphasizes how important it is for us to consider the whole person and what truly motivates people to excellence. Covey (1991) believes that the first three paradigms (authoritarian/scientific, human relations, human resource) he lists are fundamentally flawed because they do not take into account the full nature of people. In looking at the whole person, we recognize that values, principles, and ideals all appeal to the highest and best in humankind, ennobling and empowering rather than demotivating and diminishing the individual. What kind of leader is required to operate successfully within this kind of paradigm?

Recent years have seen a great deal of convergence about what makes an ideal leader, and I find the advancement of recent philosophies quite heartening. If nothing else, the popularity of particular authors who have written about leadership means that they are strik-

14

TABLE 4.1
Covey/Sergiovanni Management Paradigms

Paradigm/Source	*Principle/Assumption*	*Metaphor*	*Leadership strategy*
Authoritarian/Scientific *Bureaucratic*	Top-down control, economic motivation *Rules, low trust*	Stomach	*Check and inspect, train, compliance*
Technical-rational	*Applied science, one best way*		*Develop technicians*
Human relations	Benevolent authoritarian	Heart	Kindly, fair father
Human resource *Psychological*	Use and development of talent *Compliance due to congenial climate*	Mind	*Expect and reward workers, read people and barter successfully*
Professional	*Craft knowledge and personal expertise*		*Professional dialogue, development, discretion*
Principle-centered *Moral authority*	Meaning in work *Obligation and duty flow from shared values and ideals*	Spirit (whole person)	*Identify values, establish norms, promote collegiality and community*

NOTE: Covey (1991) is in regular type; Sergiovanni (1992) is in italic type.

ing chords of agreement in the hearts of their readers. Five aspects of successful leaders emerge from the leadership literature. These strands are inclusive and are not discussed here in order of significance. Neither are the examples given meant to be exhaustive; rather, they are representative of many other such available works.

Trusting the Leader

You can fool some people for a time, but after a while, who you are as a leader becomes obvious to all. For any kind of sustained, effective leadership, followers must be able to trust their leader. One of the most important traits in a leader is *integrity.* Followers must see integrity demonstrated by their leader. Covey (1991) mentions the importance of the development of trust at the personal and interpersonal levels. At the personal level, trustworthiness is based on character and competence. At the interpersonal level, trust refers to trustworthiness, the building of emotional "bank accounts" between people. Covey believes that "trust—or the lack of it—is at the root of success or failure in relationships and in the bottom-line results of business, industry, education, and government" (p. 31).

The person of the leader is crucial to effective leadership. Farson (1996) reiterates: "In both parenthood and management, it's not so much what we do as what we are that counts. . . People learn—and respond to—what we are" (p. 34). An old adage states that children learn more through what is caught than taught.

Who are we, really, as human beings? Sometimes as leaders we can't be fully effective until we drop our pretenses, our masks, and become vulnerable. Then, people are able to relate to us as human beings. Perhaps we need to give people "handles"—reveal our idiosyncrasies so that others have appropriate ways to show affection through good-natured teasing and to build relationships with us. As leaders, are we genuine people, or are we automatons that are always in control and have all the appropriate answers? When followers do not trust the leader, they are often fearful that the leader will manipulate them to achieve results. They may resist the leader in an attempt to make the leader come "unglued," thereby showing to all that she or he doesn't really have it all together after all. Followers want to respect the character and competence of the leader while at the same time see her or his humanness.

Once trust has been established, followers are ready to submit to the leadership of their leader because it has been based on personal power, rather than on positional power. Followers are ready to learn from, and together with, the leader they respect. Obviously, the more a leader is respected, the more personal power she or he will possess. Covey (1991) suggests that certain leadership qualities authentically increase the leader's power: persuasion, patience, gentleness, teachableness, acceptance, kindness, openness, compassionate confrontation, consistency, and integrity. Max DePree (1992) states that the entire well-being of any institution depends on the ability to trust each other and to give each other the space to achieve personal potential. Goleman (1998) believes that, among superior leaders, coaching is a crucial skill for developing others. To coach effectively, there must be an open, trusting relationship. He reports that coaches with the best results spent most of their time being positive to their pupils and only devoted about 5% of their time to confronting poor performance of their pupils. He states about the keys to success in leadership: "The best coaches show a genuine personal interest in those they guide, and have empathy for and an understanding of their employees. Trust was crucial—when there was little trust in the coach, advice went unheeded" (pp. 147-148).

Emerging evidence from emotional intelligence studies emphasizes how crucial the personal qualities of the leader have become. In an analysis of international organizations, Goleman (1990) discovered that the listed competencies for company leaders were composed of 80% to 100% emotional competencies, as opposed to technical or cognitive competencies. He goes on to list three categories of competence—two of which deal with emotional intelligence. The first category deals with personal competencies like achievement, self-confidence, and commitment. The second category deals with social competencies like influence, political awareness, and empathy. The third category is cognitive—strategic thinking, seeing the big picture and its corresponding patterns, and future thinking. What makes great leaders, in his estimation, is their use of emotional intelligence to blend information from these three competencies into a compelling vision.

Leaders build trust through who they are and how they respond to others. They must be "real people" and show vulnerability, honesty, and integrity. A positive attitude toward others and strong emotional competencies are crucial for trust and leadership success.

Passion—Heart—Soul

It is encouraging to note that we are beginning once again to recognize our spiritual side as people. Since the Age of Enlightenment, we have come to rely heavily on science for rational, analytic answers to life's questions. We are realizing and acknowledging that behaviorism and empirically proven teaching behaviors are not the complete answer to what constitutes good teachers. All the answers to life's questions cannot be explained by science. I'm not sure that even the most ardent believer in the science of teaching could ever in her or his heart completely dismiss the art of teaching. Passion, spirit, heart, soul—whatever you call it, these uniquely human, difficult-to-quantify qualities—the most effective leaders have them in spades.

As Bolman and Deal (1995) emphasize:

> The heart of leadership lies in the heart of the leader. . . [L]eaders with soul bring spirit to organizations. They marry the two, so that spirit feeds soul rather than starving it and soul enriches spirit rather than killing it. Leaders of spirit find their soul's treasure store and offer its gifts to others. (p. 10)

They point out the inadequacies of leaders with only "hands," the heroic champion with extraordinary stature and vision; and the leaders with only "heads," the skilled analyst who solves pressing problems with information, programs, and policies. Both types by themselves lack courage, spirit, and hope. Sergiovanni (1992) recognizes that the head (my mindscape of how the world works) of leadership is shaped by the heart (what I value and believe), which drives the hand (my decisions, actions, and behaviors).

Good leaders demonstrate both a high level of competence and a love for what they are about. They make their organizations places that are fueled by their passion. Positive energy from the leader energizes the group: The more positive the mood of the group leader, the more positive, helpful, and cooperative are those in the group. Goleman

(1998) reports on a U.S. Navy study that revealed the greatest difference in average and superior leaders came down to the difference in
emotional style:

> The most effective leaders were more positive and outgoing,
> more emotionally expressive and dramatic, warmer and more
> sociable (including smiling more), friendlier and more demo-
> cratic, more cooperative, more likeable and "fun to be with,"
> more appreciative and trustful, and even gentler than those
> who were merely average. By contrast the mediocre Navy lead-
> ers reflected the classic stereotype of the military taskmaster.
> They were legalistic, negative, harsh, disapproving, and ego-
> centric. (p. 188)

Likewise, the two most common traits of top executives who failed
were rigidity (inability to adapt, listen, or learn) and poor relationships
(too harshly critical, insensitive, or demanding) (Leslie & VanVelsor as
cited in Goleman, 1998). Leading with heart means leading with com-
passion and a desire for justice; if an error is made, it comes from
empathy, love, kindness, and a desire to be equitable and understanding. DePree (1992) states it eloquently: "So much of leadership
is music from the heart. . . [W]ithout understanding the cares, yearn-
ings, and struggles of the human spirit, how could anyone presume to
lead a groups of people across the street. . . [P]erson skills always pre-
cede professional skills" (p. 13). The best kind of leadership, then, is
done with passion, heart, and soul—seeking to appeal to people's values and their desire to make meaning.

Power, Pain, Participation, and Praise

How can the wise and effective leader use and retain power most effectively? It is paradoxical that usually power is gained when it is
shared with others. Farson's (1996) analogy is helpful:

> Granting authority is not like handing out a piece of pie,
> wherein you lose what you give away. It is more like what hap-
> pens when you give information to someone. Although he or
> she may now know more, you do not know any less. (p. 22)

In the process, you have probably added to the trust level between the
two persons. The receiver is honored to be given the responsibility
and feels further allegiance and loyalty back to the giver. The hoarding
of power dampens the spirit.

Stripped of power, people look for ways to fight back . . . giving power liberates energy for more productive use. When people feel a sense of efficacy and an ability to influence their world, they seek to be productive. They direct their energy and intelligence toward making a contribution rather than obstructing progress. (Bolman & Deal, 1995, p. 107)

Sergiovanni (1992) reminds us of the importance of Greenleaf's enduring concept of *servant leadership* (developed from Biblical principles taught and exemplified by Jesus). Servant leadership provides the legitimacy to lead. Followers of a servant leader follow because they believe that the leader makes leadership judgments on the basis of competence and values, rather than on self-interest. Servant leadership seeks to clarify shared values and to empower decision making based on the community covenant of values. Servant leaders "don't inflict pain, they bear it" (DePree, 1989). As a leader, DePree asked himself: "Am I inadvertently bruising the spirit or obstructing the performance of the people for whom I am responsible?" (p. 221). DePree (1989) defined the art of leadership as "liberating people to do what is required of them in the most effective and humane way possible." The servant leader seeks to remove "obstacles that keep them from doing their jobs . . . and enables his or her followers to realize their full potential."

The move to participatory management is an attempt to develop people and to share responsibility with them. DePree believes that participatory management is the most effective contemporary management practice because it begins with a belief in the potential of people. Schlechty (1990) emphasizes that a participatory leader is not authoritarian, laissez-faire, or democratic, but rather is "strong enough to trust others with his or her fate, just as he or she expects their trust in return" (p. 129). Effective leaders do not view control as the issue, but trust the wisdom of the group. "Their strength is not in control alone, but in other qualities—passion, sensitivity, tenacity, patience, courage, firmness, enthusiasm, and wonder" (Farson, 1996, p. 38). Farson (1996) also found, through studying how power is achieved in a group, that most often those who served the group rather than dominated it were the ones who emerged as the leader. Servant leaders build on the successes of each individual in the group and help them achieve their potential.

How do leaders bring out the best in others? Do they give a lot of "positive strokes"? How do they use criticism? Goleman (1995) cites the work of Harry Levinson, a psychoanalyst-turned-corporate-consultant, who suggests that the art of praise and the art of critique are closely intertwined. He suggests that, for either praise or critique to be effective, a leader must also be specific, offer a solution, be present (do it in person rather than by memo), and be sensitive. Farson questions the motivational value of praise and warns:

- Praise may, in fact, be perceived as threatening

- Instead of reassuring people about their worth, praise may be a way of gaining status over them

- Praise may constrict creativity rather than free it

- Praise can come to be associated mainly with criticism

- Rather than function as a bridge between people, praise may actually put distance between them

- Rather than opening the way to further contact, praise may be a way of terminating it

Sadly, praise has lost credibility because it has been used for so many purposes other than expressing genuine appreciation. Leaders must be careful how they use both praise and critique; it all goes back to the issue of credibility and trust.

The Leader's View of the Followers

Also significant in the relationship between leader and followers is the way the leader views the followers. The leader's perspective must be based on respect for each person. We may not like all those we lead, but we must be willing to accept them and to respond in affirming ways. Basically, the literature tells us that the followers' perception of how much the leader likes, respects, and seeks the best for them is extremely important. Covey (1991) has come to believe that "whatever view we have of people is self-fulfilling" (p. 201).

What is the first step toward gaining a positive view of followers? Seek first to understand and appreciate them for who they are. The job of the leader is to seek out understanding, help followers build on their strengths, and provide opportunities where their gifts can be developed. Appreciating what others bring builds genuine trust and helps us be honest as well in admitting the things we don't know or can't do. This assessment of our limitations helps us recognize that we need each other and encourages us to practice the Japanese proverb "All of us are smarter than any one of us." Jack Welch, CEO of General Electric, speaks of valuing people: "The most important thing a leader has to do is absolutely search and treasure and nourish the voice and dignity of every person. It is in the end the key element" (as quoted in Slater, 1999, p. 163).

Bringing Out the Best in Others

When we value people and the gifts they bring to an organization, we are starting out with the right attitude and heart-set, but how can we help others achieve and really reach their potential?

Respecting people as individuals means that we work with each person differently. Drucker (1998) notes that although the evidence for this approach has been overwhelming, relatively little attention has been paid to the idea. He also points out that the role and responsibility of the worker has changed significantly, and he coined the term "knowledge worker" to conceptualize the difference. He describes a knowledge worker as a worker who knows more about her or his job than anybody else in the organization. This is true even when the worker is in a subordinate role to a higher authority. The relationship is "more like that between the conductor of an orchestra and the people who play the instruments. The conductor may not even know how to play the violin, yet the success of his conducting depends upon the quality of his associates" (p. 164). What is Drucker's advice for leaders? He suggests: "One does not 'manage' people, as previously assumed. One leads them. The way one maximizes their performance is by capitalizing on their strengths and their knowledge rather than trying to force them into molds" (p. 166). One of my favorite quotes on this subject is from Jack Welch, CEO of General Electric: "We have to undo a 100-year-old concept and convince our managers that their role is not to control and stay on top of things, but to guide, energize, and excite." It seems to me that a classroom teacher is a rather perfect description of a knowledge worker. Who knows more about the classroom culture, the individuals and group dynamics that compose that culture, the practical wisdom relative to that age-group, and the command of the particular subject matter for that discipline and age-group than the classroom teacher?

It is also becoming clearer that the climate we set for how people work together is very important. Deming (as cited in Holt, 1993) argues: "The way people work together is what produces excellence . . . the climate of an organization influences an individual's contribution more than the individual himself" (p. 329). Darling-Hammond (1997) underscores this point:

> Successful 21st-century schools will be grounded on two very different presumptions: first, that teaching matters and, second, that relationships matter . . . no individual can possibly know everything there is to know about teaching. Only when principals and teachers pool their energies and share their knowledge in a professional culture can continual progress be made. (p. 1)

What personal traits or competencies do we need to encourage in followers so that they can develop their own gifts and work well with others? During the last quarter century of research, Goleman (1998) contends, a common core of personal and social abilities is the key: emotional intelligence. In his words, *emotional intelligence* is "the capacity for recognizing our own feelings and those of others, for motivating ourselves, and for managing emotions well in ourselves and in our relationships" (p. 317). Goleman believes that IQ, experience, and expertise are significant but that what really separates excellent performers is their degree of self-awareness, self-regulation, motivation, empathy, and social skills—that is, their emotional intelligence.

When we think of teachers as knowledge workers, how can we earn enthusiasm and commitment from them? What considerations and processes should be put in place to maximize results? We must do significant things together as leader and followers. We must ask them to do significant and meaningful work with their colleagues and us. As human beings, we all want to be a part of efforts that are purposeful, to make a contribution, and to make the world a better place. Bolman and Deal (1995) suggest that we must give authorship—"space within boundaries"—so that, through trusting people to solve problems and make meaningful contributions, we increase enthusiasm, sense of control, and commitment. As leaders, we are responsible to create the kinds of conditions and processes where authorship can occur. We must learn to open ourselves to trust the individual and the group. Farson (1996) states:

> Participative management—involving the people who have to do the work in the decisions that will affect them—is based upon the idea that people are better than we think they are and can be counted on to make wise choices. A considerable amount of research shows that people learn faster, produce more, and are more highly motivated when participative methods are employed. The challenge for management is to tap this powerful resource. (p. 78)

Administrators need to create a learning culture within schools, a safe place where the gifts and strengths of each individual can be maximized, where authorship can occur, and where individuals can work together with others, developing their emotional intelligence and finding meaning in what they create. As leaders, we must take the risk to trust, to think and expect the best, and to use the minds of our followers. We must excite and inspire our followers, building enthusiasm and commitment. We must be the leaders of the band because "jazz, like leadership, combines the unpredictability of the future with the gifts of individuals" (DePree, 1992, p. 9). In the next chapter, we explore how we can better understand our band members to make the most beautiful music possible.

CHAPTER FIVE

Motivation, Learning, and Staff Development

What Motivates Teachers?

To continue the analogy from the Chapter 4, why do people want to play in the band and make music, anyway? We have looked at the role the leader of the band plays, and now we turn to the performers as individuals and as a group. Why do teachers enter the profession? What brings meaning and joy to their work? We must find out what motivates them if we hope to work with them collaboratively and successfully.

Are teachers motivated by money? The past two decades have seen many efforts at improving teacher performance through greater financial rewards. These rewards have included merit pay, career ladders, and other types of incentive plans. Many of these reforms came out of political initiatives designed to increase teacher accountability and motivation. Cornett (1995) reports that merit pay plans were mostly met with opposition from teachers and teacher unions and have met with limited acceptance. Renyi (1998) found, after questioning nearly 1,000 teachers in a National Foundation for the Improvement of Education survey, that only 5% of teachers were motivated to grow professionally so that they could make more money. Drucker (1998) concurs: "We have known for 50 years that money alone does not motivate employees to perform much more than it motivates volunteers."

What are superintendents' perceptions regarding pay and other motivators, such as tenure or competency tests, in motivating teachers and improving the quality of teaching? In a survey of 622 superintendents by the Gordon S. Black Corporation, only 37% thought linking pay to student performance was an excellent or good idea, and 63% thought it was a fair or poor idea. Similarly, on linking tenure with student performance, 66% considered it a fair or poor idea, and on requiring teachers to take competency tests, 65% thought it a poor or fair idea (Archer, 1998b). The American public likewise has little faith in the ability of money to motivate; only 18% in a 1998 Association for Supervision and Curriculum Development (ASCD) public opinion poll preferred improving teacher performance by linking salary with student performance (Willis, 1998).

What attracts educators to the profession? Topping the list as teacher motivators in the National Foundation survey were (a) to improve student achievement (73%), (b) to improve teaching skills (55%), and (c) to increase knowledge (34%). Sergiovanni (1992) cites two studies (Lortie and Johnson) that indicate a sense of altruism permeates the commitment to the profession. Lortie's study reported that people entered the profession to serve others, to work with students, for the enjoyment of the job itself, for material benefits, and because of the school calendar. In Johnson's interviews of 100 teachers, the responses centered on the following themes: a calling, a sense of mission, and commitment to professional, social, or religious ideals. In my experience in education, I have seen that most educators enter the profession because of a sincere desire to work with children and to help them succeed.

The Teacher as Professional

Previous chapters have discussed the significance of the leader's role in setting up structures and processes to involve followers in meaning-making work. The intention is to promote efficacy in people—that is, the belief that they can produce the intended or desired result in their work. Ultimately, we should seek to build leadership capacity in people so that as their sense of professionalism and efficacy increases, the need for direct supervision and leadership will decrease. Contrast the growth in efficacy between a new, inexperienced teacher and a veteran teacher; leadership capacity has been increased.

We expect teachers to grow as professionals as they progress and gain experience in their work. Lambert (1998) describes professional educators as "learners who attend to the learning of both adults and children" (p. 92). She notes that developing leadership capacity in educators goes beyond shared decision making and includes five crucial features: (a) broad-based, skillful participation, (b) inquiry-based use of information to inform decisions and practice, (c) roles and responsibilities that reflect broad involvement and collaboration, (d) reflective practice and innovation as the norm, and (e) high student achievement. Glasser (1993) describes the difference between a nonprofessional and a professional as a quality that goes far beyond a person needing supervision to do a good job. He views the professional as someone who always strives to perform with quality and therefore continually seeks to improve the way the job is done, both individually and collegially. As leaders, we must view teachers as professionals and encourage them to view themselves as professionals as

well. Bolman and Deal (1995) believe that "when people feel a sense
of efficacy and an ability to influence their world, they seek to be
productive. They direct their energy and intelligence toward making
a contribution rather than obstructing progress" (p. 107).

The Professional Teacher and
the Role of the Leader

What should the relationship look like between the leader and the
teacher as professional? It should always seek to allow the teacher to
function as much as a professional as possible. Glasser (1993) believes
that as long as teachers operate in traditional schools and have administrators, boards, state departments, and legislatures telling them what
to do, they will not have much of a chance to behave as true professionals, such as physicians or lawyers do. Sergiovanni (1992) describes professionalism as competence plus virtue. Competent educational professionals are always self-directed in their learning, just as
competent doctors are continually keeping abreast of the knowledge
base and seeking to expand their own knowledge. They also are purposeful at being self-reflective about their own practice, they try new
approaches, and they take responsibility to share insights and results
with other colleagues. In summarizing the work of McIntyre, Flores, and
Noddings, Sergiovanni describes professional virtue as being made up
of four dimensions: (a) a commitment to practice in an exemplary
way, (b) a commitment to practice toward valued social ends, (c) a
commitment not only to one's own practice but also to the practice
itself, and (d) a commitment to the ethic of caring. Our goal as leaders
should be to hold out an expectation of professionalism and to seek to
nurture and develop it in each teacher. What we know about how people are motivated and what brings out excellence moves us as leaders
farther and farther from the dependency model of teachers working
for rewards and a what-gets-rewarded-gets-done mentality.

The Teacher as Adult Learner

If we are to move toward a more effective evaluation and professional
growth plan for teachers, it is essential that we understand how teachers learn best. What types of experiences have the most impact on
teacher beliefs and subsequent teaching practice? Is what we have
done during the past 20 years an effective way to develop our teachers
and affect instructional practice? Ultimately, we should seek to develop a process and activities that are meaningful to teachers and that

significantly affect the ways instruction is delivered so we can reach our goal of increasing student achievement. Knowles (as cited by Dreyfuss in Glickman, 1992) advances four assumptions of adult learning as applied to supervision:

1. Processes should recognize adults as autonomous and self-directing.

2. Adults' rich backgrounds and expertise can be applied to educational issues through the process.

3. Readiness for learning is determined by each individual's unique circumstances in his or her professional practice. Supervisors must assist with actual and perceptual reality issues.

4. Adult involvement will vary according to the immediacy of application of newly acquired abilities and insights. Adults will be committed to an *effective* supervisory process and understand how it relates to their current professional lives.

Connect Learning

Research tells us that adults learn much as students do. Lieberman (1995) reports that people learn best through active involvement and articulating what they have learned. Have we given these kinds of opportunities to our teachers, or have we assumed that if we expose teachers to concepts in an in-service that somehow those ideas will be translated into practice? Have we involved teachers in meaningful follow-up, asked them to think through what they learned, and then helped them apply it to their situation? My judgment is that we have not set up processes or structures or allowed the time for appropriate interaction on new learning that has been presented. I have seen too many "one size fits all" presentations without opportunity given for teachers to wrestle with concepts and ideas and to embed them into practice. We have also been guilty of "covering" a topic and then moving on to the next hot topic, much like those teachers who stress "inch-deep coverage" at the expense of "mile-deep learning." We need to take a long-term approach to staff development and seek to connect people in meaningful ways so that together they can integrate the new information presented to them.

In reflecting on a project that increased teacher development through collegiality, Ponticell (1995) makes six powerful points about teacher learning:

1. Teachers learn when they perceive a personal need for change—risk taking following an examination of their own teaching.

2. Teacher learning is context specific—sorting out what works in their teaching environment.

3. Teachers are more willing to look at and change classroom practices when they are instrumental in designing and taking charge of their own professional growth activities; enhanced efficacy leads to greater expenditure of time and effort, whether paid or not.

4. Sustained, substantive, and structured collegial interactions enhance mutuality and support risk taking; the process set up for interaction is vital.

5. Learning occurs over time.

6. Teachers' professionalism is validated by commitment and support from the building principal, central office, and university in trusting teachers to take control of their own professional growth.

What comes through in the above points is the need for professionalism, self-direction, collegial interaction, and trust extended by authority figures. Any effective evaluation and professional growth plan must include these elements if it is to have a sustained chance for success. Perkins's (1992) *Theory One* about teaching and learning is both simple and profound: "People learn much of what they have a reasonable opportunity and motivation to learn" (p. 45). Perkins lists four conditions for students that I believe are also applicable to professional growth for adults: (a) clear information about goals, knowledge needed, and performances expected; (b) thoughtful practice; (c) informative feedback; and (d) strong motivation. Do our current systems of learning for teachers' professional growth include these elements?

Apply Wisdom

We need to help people develop mind-sets based on principles instead of practices based on policies (Covey, 1991). Principle-based learning guides and empowers people to think for themselves as they apply principles to various situations, whereas practice-based learning depends on rules and regulations that may work in one situation but not another. For example, as consumers we become frustrated in retail stores and other customer service situations when policies are applied versus the salesperson looking at us as human beings and applying commonsense principles to resolve a difficulty. Given the complexity of teaching and the need for the application of wisdom in a variety of situations, we must encourage principle-based thinking and the development of habits of the mind in our teachers.

Develop Emotional Intelligence

Goleman's (1998) work points out the significance of the development of emotional intelligence in both predicting long-term success and total effectiveness. Emotional competencies were found to be twice as important as intelligence as measured by IQ or expertise in determining a given profile of excellence. Goleman also cites a study by Buchele that found that the higher the level of the job, the less important technical and cognitive abilities were, and the more important competence in emotional intelligence became. I believe that this new information about the "soft skills" we need to encourage in teachers has significant applications as we consider how best to assist them with learning and how we work with them in evaluation. Our traditional evaluation systems have devalued the emotional intelligence of our teachers and have valued technical and cognitive answers to teaching and learning.

We know that our traditional methods have also been based on a system of diagnosing a problem and a system of following policy rather than encouraging principle-based thinking and the development of one's sense of efficacy. To build self-confidence and develop efficacy in our teachers, we must put into place processes and systems that express confidence and trust, that give meaning and motivation to the teacher, if we are to maximize adult learning in our schools. Our goal in staff development should be the ideal adult learning situation that Schlechty (1990, drawing on the work of Kelley) describes:

> Every day it is expected that all will manage themselves well without supervision, that they will be committed to the purpose for which schools exist. . . [T]hey will continuously build their competence and focus their effort in ways that are designed to produce optimal results for students . . . and that they will provide leaders and others with the feedback they need rather than the feedback they want. (p. 11)

Given the rapid rate of change we will find ourselves dealing with in the 21st century, we must move our teachers into a mode of continuous improvement, innovation, and refinement of teaching and learning or else we lose ground. An attitude and environment of continuous improvement and learning is simply nonnegotiable. But to build communities where this attitude is the norm, we must make significant links between individual evaluation and growth and the development of our staff and school as a whole.

The Linkage Between Individual Development and Staff Development

How can we reflect best practice in our professional growth and evaluation systems? Professional development must be both linked with individual needs and developed through a comprehensive plan by system shareholders. A push-pull relationship exists between the individual and system needs; sometimes one will drive the other and vice versa. For example, a system decision to increase an emphasis on diversity may push some teachers' individual development plans, or teachers may be involved in having their awareness increased through curricular or system committee work. Individual development and growth, however, may raise new understandings that move a school or system toward more effective strategies. As several teachers express a desire to learn about a new topic or seek training to remediate a perceived weakness, the whole system may be moved in a previously unanticipated direction. Professional development can therefore be directive or directed.

The value of a systematic, coherent plan for a district or school is desirable but should not be so rigid that flexibility is sacrificed in this time of rapid change. In either case, we are realizing the importance of follow-up in the teacher's work situation, that the development is job-embedded (Sparks, 1997). We know from past experience that much of our staff development effort in teaching strategies and curriculum resulted in as few as 10% of those participating actually implementing what they had learned (Showers & Joyce, 1996). We need to expect staff development trainers not only to train but also to follow-up with consultation and facilitation.

We must place greater emphasis on development of teacher expertise, rather than expect it to come from an expert and appropriate time given for the work to be done. Teacher involvement in staff development at the district or individual level is crucial to long-term success. Successful staff development must continually be focused on the needs of the learner at the school level and be results-driven (Sparks & Hirsch, 1997). Collegial settings such as study groups, action research, peer coaching, curriculum development, and case discussion provide opportunities for teacher growth. Traditional assumptions are more likely to be challenged in collegial groups, and this type of staff development is more likely to have an impact on student learning.

Although many needs are met through the model described above, for collegial and system professional development, many needs remain that must be addressed through attention to individual needs.

Because of differences in teachers' needs and experience levels, Quinn (1998) suggests a differentiated model of professional development. He emphasizes the principles of professionalism, an atmosphere of mutual trust between supervisor and teacher, growth as a journey, growth and not evaluation as a priority, introspective reflection and self-analysis as being crucial ingredients, and a tailored program for each teacher's needs.

In Figure 5.1, I show how teacher evaluation, professional development, and curriculum development and implementation are all linked in individual and system ways. Each area has a significant impact on student achievement and needs to operate in a climate of continuous school improvement.

Continuous School Improvement

Continuous school improvement in all three areas is driven by four main factors:

1. *Board and administration*—who guide systemic evaluation, strategic planning, and the mission and vision of the organization

2. *Parents and community*—who provide informal feedback through daily evaluation and formal feedback through such means as surveys and focus groups

3. *State and federal issues*—such as accreditation, development of standards and assessments, and legislative mandates

4. *Faculty*—who engage in best practices, reflection, dialogue, study, action research, and development of new learning and ideas

Teaching, Learning, and Curriculum Development— Professional Development

Moving to the inner part of the circle in Figure 5.1, teaching, learning, and curriculum development are on the top of the triangle because it is the reason schools exist. As I described earlier, a direct relationship exists between teaching, learning, and curriculum development and professional development. Curriculum development happens informally each time a teacher plans a lesson for students. Teacher effectiveness in the implementation of the lesson, or lack thereof, flows from the level of professional development or proficiency inherent in the teacher. Staff development on both an individual and systemic level for the individual teacher has a profound impact on the delivery of instruction at the individual level and also in terms of that teacher being able to participate effectively in any systemwide curriculum de-

Continuous School Improvement

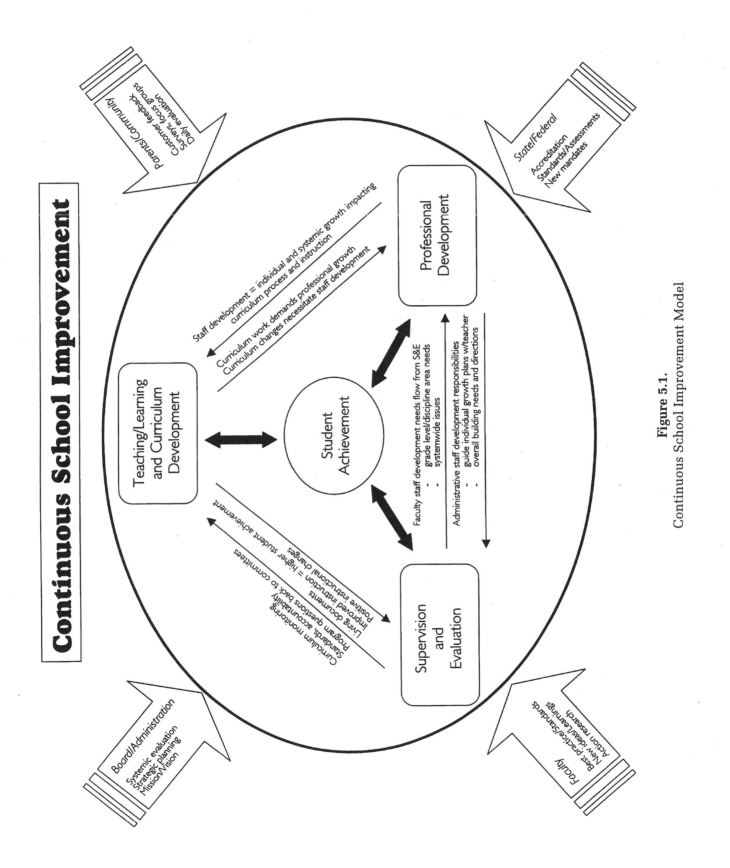

Student Achievement

Teaching/Learning and Curriculum Development

Professional Development

Supervision and Evaluation

Staff development = individual and systemic growth impacting curriculum process and instruction

Curriculum work demands professional growth
Curriculum changes necessitate staff development

Faculty staff development needs flow from S&E
- grade level/discipline area needs
- systemwide issues

Administrative staff development responsibilities
- guide individual growth plans w/teacher
- overall building needs and directions

Curriculum monitoring
Standards accountability
Program questions back to committees
Living documents = higher student achievement
Improved instruction = positive instructional changes

Parents/Community
Customer feedback
Survey, focus groups
Daily evaluation

State/Federal
Accreditation
Standards/Assessments
New mandates

Board/Administration
Systemic evaluation
Strategic planning
Mission/Vision

Faculty
Best practice/Standards
New ideas/Learnings
Action research

Figure 5.1.
Continuous School Improvement Model

velopment. Curriculum work demands further professional growth by committee members to solve problems and fully articulate a curriculum. Teachers bring their own learning from their teaching experiences and past professional growth to bear on the curriculum process. Furthermore, curricular changes (new resources, strategies) necessitate staff development activities for those not involved on the particular curriculum committee that has recommended changes. This staff development achieved through individual or larger group processes results in individual and system growth, which in turn again affects the curriculum process and instructional practice.

Professional Development—Supervision and Evaluation

Administrators must take responsibility to provide various forms of guidance for individual teachers' development at whatever stage of their career. As administrators are in touch with teachers' growth, needs for professional development will arise on an individual and system basis. These needs must be met by continuous professional development. The guiding maxim must be "Improved instruction equals higher student achievement and success." As administrators are concerned with the continuous learning or professional development of the individual and the school community, they will seek out ways to assist in meeting individual needs through disseminating appropriate professional growth opportunities. They will also take the lead in discerning overall building needs and directions.

Supervision and Evaluation—Teaching, Learning, and Curriculum Development

The responsibility for supervision and evaluation provides a platform for administrators to have significant discussions about the teaching and learning process. They bring accountability just by nature of the position they hold, but beyond that, they need to assist the teacher in having important conversations about classroom instruction. Curriculum work offers administrators the opportunity to have meaningful involvement; although they may not be the content area experts, they can give help in the process aspects of curriculum development. The type of evaluation and professional growth system described in Chapter 7 will do much to help teachers institute positive instructional changes with maximum teacher ownership and meaningful involvement by the principal. The principal also needs to be in touch with the teachers to facilitate the ongoing evaluation of the current curricular program. The principal is an important key in assisting with new curriculum implementation, as well as in identifying weaknesses in the current curriculum. Questions about curricular deficiencies need to be routed back to curriculum committees for further consideration.

As you can see from the model, the three areas of (a) teaching, learning, and curriculum development, (b) professional development, and (c) supervision and evaluation are inextricably linked. We must continue to make significant strides in each of these areas and understand the value of the connectedness between all three areas. I propose that although principals are not the instructional leaders in the sense that they are all-knowing content specialists, they still have very important and vital roles to play in all three areas. Changing our practices in the area of supervision and evaluation will help unleash to an even greater degree professional growth, reflection, collaboration, and lasting, effective change on the part of our teachers.

The Principal as Staff Developer

The significance of the role of the principal cannot be underestimated in the life of the school. Whether overtly expressed or not, the values the leader holds will be evident to the followers and will set the tone for the level of professionalism demonstrated by the faculty. Studies since the 1970s have pointed out the significant impact a principal can have. In an *Education Week* article, Keller (1998) points out that despite a growing body of research citing the principal as a major key to school improvement, no corresponding change has taken place in principal behavior. Unfortunately, some principals still have not made the connection between teacher growth and the success of their school. The 10-year study by the National Association of Elementary School Principals (Doud & Keller, 1998) on the elementary and middle school principalship reveals that whereas principals established staff supervision and contact as their highest priority, they made planning and conducting staff development one of their lowest priorities! Additionally, about half reported that their greatest need for staff development was in understanding and using technology, whereas only a third named improving staff and student performance or other school improvement issues as their greatest developmental needs. Keller reports that, on a survey, California principals wished they could spend twice as much time as they currently do on curriculum and instruction issues. Only about a quarter of their time now is devoted to teaching and school improvement. What qualities are needed for principals to be successful staff developers and change agents in their schools?

Drucker (1998) suggests that, for starters, we should view knowledge workers as associates, as partners with us. He points out that partners cannot be ordered (they need to be persuaded) and that, therefore, managing people demands marketing skills. As principals, we need to convince teachers of the significance of the mission and purpose of our organizations, provide continuous training, and help them see results. We need to create an empowering culture for them— promote their growth and collaboration with others, give options, not mandates, and help them be constructors of their own knowledge. We must give people space to grow and freedom to exercise the gifts they have been given. Comparisons breed insecurity, and we need to remember to compare people against their own potential and constantly affirm that potential and their efforts toward reaching it (Covey, 1991).

It is up to us to maintain a positive forward momentum and help those who follow see the value of continuous improvement. Our vision must be based on the ideal, and we must inspire others to pursue that vision with us. With principle-centered leaders, Covey (1991) states, "the challenge is to be a light, not a judge; to be a model, not a critic" (p. 25). Sparks (1997) emphasizes the role of principal as "system designer" of structures and systems that promote a high level of learning, performance, and results and as models who demonstrate the same level of commitment to change that they expect of their followers. The National Commission on Teaching and America's Future provides this excellent summary paragraph regarding the preparation of tomorrow's principals:

> Principals must know how to lead organizations in which leadership and decision making are shared, and continual learning is fostered for staff and parents as well as students. In a learning organization, the primary job of management is professional development . . . teaching and learning. To lead the schools of the future, principals will need to appreciate adult learning and development as well as that of children and know how to nurture a collaborative environment that fosters continual self-assessment. They will also need to be able to envision and enact new organizational arrangements in schools so that time, staffing patterns, and relationships between teachers and among teachers, students, and families better serve the goals of serious learning and high-quality teaching. (cited in Darling-Hammond, 1997, p. 3)

Development of the Total Learning Community

As leaders, we should seek to build an ethos of learning through our work with individuals and through the structures and processes we set up to guide individuals and groups. The most powerful manifestation of a total learning community is when each person takes responsibility for his or her own learning and the learning of others in the group. The processes we set up can either promote or inhibit learning. Traditional systems emphasized comparisons and competition, thereby dividing people and encouraging self-interest. Changing our evaluation systems makes a powerful statement to our teachers about our expectations and values. It can be an essential first step in changing the culture of a school to become a community of learners.

It is an accepted fact that people function more intelligently working together than individually. Barth (cited in Perkins, 1992) suggests three categories of teacher development: (a) Group 1 teachers resist change, self-reflection, and help from others; (b) Group 2 teachers reflect on their own classroom practice but resist observers getting involved; and (c) Group 3 teachers are reflective and welcome collegial interaction. We need to move all our teachers to the Group 3 level.

According to research studies, ideal school leadership consists of high degrees of leadership, skillfulness, participation, schoolwide collaboration, and emphasis on learning (Lambert, 1998). Schools with strong professional communities were more effective in promoting student achievement (Newmann & Wehlage, as cited in Lambert, 1998). Collegiality spells improvements for teachers and students: gains in achievement; higher quality solutions to problems; increased confidence among all school community members; teachers' ability to support one another's strengths and to accommodate weaknesses; ability to examine and test new ideas, methods, and materials; more systematic assistance to beginning teachers; and an expanded pool of ideas, materials, and methods (Little, as cited in Schmoker, 1996). Business theorists such as Peters, Senge, Deming, Drucker, and Welch all advocate for the creation of learning cultures. Goleman (1998) notes that teamwork and collaboration, not competition, set the outstanding performers apart from all others. As leaders and followers, we need to be learners together (DePree, 1989).

What should be our focus with teachers as we work to develop effective teams? Goleman (1998) cites the work of Drukat's analysis of 150 teams and notes these characteristics of effective teams:

- Empathy, or interpersonal understanding

- Cooperation and a unified effort

- Open communication, setting explicit norms and expectations, and confronting underperforming team members

- A drive to improve so that the team paid attention to performance feedback and sought to learn to do better

- Self-awareness, in the form of evaluating their strengths and weaknesses as a team

- Initiative and taking a proactive stance toward solving problems

- Self-confidence as a team

- Flexibility in how they went about their collective work

TABLE 5.1
Law of the Farm Principles Applied to the School Community

Covey's Law of the Farm	Life in the School Community
Prepare the ground	Develop a positive school culture and values, clearly state mission and beliefs
Put in the seed	Hire quality faculty and staff
Cultivate	Develop effective relationships and community building
Weed	Regularly perform formative and summative evaluation processes
Water	Provide staff development on an individual and group basis
*Fertilize (to maintain soil quality)	Provide self-renewing practices that maintain a learning community

NOTE: *Not listed by Covey, but was added by a former farm boy who appreciates its value.

- Organizational awareness in terms of both assessing the need of other key groups in the company and being resourceful in using what the organization had to offer

- Building bonds to other teams

Once again, we see the need for development of emotional intelligence in our teachers. What we are learning from brain research is that emotions take precedence over reason. How we develop people in these areas will be an important priority as we move toward increased collegiality and a higher level of professionalism. As we move toward being a "placeless" society, "effective leaders will be constantly sifting for ideas that can bring people and resources together. . . [T]he success of any organization will fundamentally depend on its people" (Knoke, 1996, p. 51). Knoke (1996) notes that because of technology's multiplier effect, ethical or moral breakdowns will severely handicap organizational effectiveness. Sergiovanni (1992) urges that we must build strong covenants of values (moral authority) with groups to have effective leadership capacity.

In conclusion, I believe that Covey's (1991) law of the farm principles can be developed into an excellent metaphor for professional life in the school setting (see Table 5.1).

In our attempts to reach the goals stated above, it is clearly our responsibility to explore new approaches that will help our teachers and students achieve to their fullest potential and use the gifts they have been given. We explore the promises and pitfalls of new forms of teacher evaluation and professional growth in the next chapter. I also propose a practical system that has shown excellent results.

PART II

CHAPTER SIX

New Approaches to Evaluation and Staff Development

Factors Supporting New Approaches

Teacher evaluation is currently in a state of flux, but I view this as an exciting time to be an administrator. Advancements in technology and research are uncovering and confirming the optimum ways in which people learn. New approaches are encouraging because educators recognize the need for (a) a stronger emphasis on the humanity or art of teaching while maintaining the appropriate balance of good science, (b) a greater focus on students and their learning, and (c) better ways to work together cooperatively toward common goals as administrators and teachers.

In previous chapters, I have attempted to demonstrate the following points supporting a new method of teacher evaluation and growth:

- Teachers have powerful effects on student learning. Consequently, administrators should focus their energies on teachers if they want to affect student achievement.

- Teaching is a very complex activity and is not reducible to a set of teaching behaviors.

- Supervision and evaluation have several aspects, and the role of principal as sole evaluator has serious limitations.

- Teachers and principals agree about the ineffectiveness of past supervisory approaches.

- Supervisory approaches have shifted from bureaucratic authority to technical authority to a blend of professional and moral authority.

- The person of the leader is a key ingredient in creating a culture of learning and growth.

- We need to find out what motivates teachers to grow; then, we need to design systems that incorporate those principles.

- How we view teachers as professionals and adult learners determines what kinds of structures and processes we set up.

- Structures and processes need to show strong links among supervision and evaluation, professional development, and teaching and learning.

- The principal plays a key role by being an example and in designing systems that enhance and encourage teacher growth.

Additionally, we are in the process of changing our perspectives on teaching and learning from traditional views to an increasing emphasis on a constructivist approach. Even though a balance of views is desirable, I believe that the constructivist approach is gaining ascendancy because this way of teaching helps learning "stick" better, and it is a response to the increasingly fragmented and complex explosion of information occurring in our society. We need to give students tools and processes to help them make sense of the information they are receiving. A fixed body of knowledge in the traditional model is less certain because of rapid change; processes and models for thinking become more important than reproduction of knowledge shared by the teacher. Nolan and Francis (as cited in Glickman, 1992) argue that this shift in teaching approach has significance for how we provide supervision:

- Teachers should be viewed as active constructors of their own knowledge about learning and teaching.

- Supervisors should be viewed as collaborators in creating knowledge about teaching and learning.

- The variety of data sources used to capture pertinent information should be increased.

- Both general principles and methods of teaching, as well as content-specific principles and methods, must be considered.

- Supervision should become more group oriented than individual oriented.

Teachers must be expected to construct meaning from experiences and to form a plan for future growth and direction in cooperation with their administrator. With the move to participatory management and site-based decision making, teachers are viewed as decision makers and play a larger role in determining the professional growth they need, as opposed to receiving it in a top-down manner (Glickman, 1992). The explosion of knowledge and information has grown exponentially and will continue to grow. Kelley (as cited in Goleman, 1998) estimates, on the basis of his studies, that as compared with 1986, when workers had about 75% of the knowledge they needed to do their jobs, in 1997, workers had 10% to 15% of that knowledge. This fact leads to an increased need for collaboration as knowledge workers. The rate of change necessitates that teachers and students develop flexibility, adaptability, and an ability to deal with change. Principals similarly need flexible processes that allow them to be in touch continuously with teachers and to assist them in their change and growth plans.

The Need for Reflective Practice and Self-Assessment

If you think about the most effective teachers on your staff, you will probably discover that they are also the best at self-assessment skills because they have practiced them for years. It is important that before we begin to explore new approaches being tried in supervision and evaluation, we understand the significance of the habits of reflection on practice and continuous self-assessment. The new approaches all depend in some way on teacher self-assessment skills. Schlechty (1990) calls self-evaluation "the most powerful form of evaluation" (p. 115).

How should self-assessment be done? Airasian and Gullickson's (1997) work at the Center for Research on Accountability and Teacher Evaluation (CREATE) at Western Michigan University has been stimulating to my thinking and the development of the Growth-Focused Evaluation System. They list four steps that teachers go through while informally or formally conducting self-evaluation:

1. *Problem Identification:* Teachers identify a problem or question about their practice that they are motivated to address.

2. *Information Gathering:* They collect data to inform the area of practice.

3. *Reflection and Decision Making:* After reflection and analysis of the data, teachers make meaning from them.

4. *Application and Change:* Plans are made to carry out changes in practice.

Why is it so important that teachers engage in self-evaluation? Airasian and Gullickson (1997) list eight reasons why self-evaluation is an important process to use in formative evaluation:

1. It is a professional responsibility.

2. It focuses professional development and improvement on the classroom or school level where teachers have their greatest expertise and effect.

3. It recognizes that organizational change is usually the result of individuals changing themselves and their personal practices, not of "top-down" mandates.

4. It gives teachers voice—that is, a stake in and control over their own practice.

5. It makes teachers aware of the strengths and weaknesses of their practice; it grows from the immediacy and complexity of the classroom, as do teachers' motives and incentives.

6. It encourages ongoing teacher development and discourages unchanging classroom beliefs, routine, and methods.

7. It treats the teacher as a professional and can improve teacher morale and motivation.

8. It encourages collegial interactions and discussions about teaching. (Airasian & Gullickson, 1994; McCloskey & Egelson, 1993)

Lambert (1998) holds up reflective practice as a crucial aspect of building high leadership capacity into schools and emphasizes the need to give appropriate time for such activities. Quality in an organization can only be achieved if all learn to evaluate their own work and are trusted to do so by management (Glasser, 1992). Perkins (1992) says that all the extensive research on human thinking and learning can be boiled down to one sentence: *"Learning is a consequence of thinking.* Retention, understanding, and the active use of knowledge can be brought about only by learning experiences in which learners think about and think with what they are learning" (p. 8). Of course, this statement applies to teachers and administrators, as well as to students. Top performers show a passion for feedback in the self-evaluation process:

> For many people getting performance feedback can be frustratingly difficult because of the unquantifiable nature of their work. Such people have to develop a strong self-critical sense, to provide the feedback themselves. And top performers seek out the feedback they need at the point when it is most useful to them. (Goleman, 1998, p. 67)

How can administrators encourage self-reflective practice in schools? Patterson (1993) lists three key criteria:

1. Leaders create an environment of safety so that all employees can freely express their thoughts without fear of intimidation or recrimination. Leaders establish trust and safety nets.

2. Leaders should learn to separate the person from the issue. Leaders keep the reflection on issues, not on people.

3. Individuals develop the capacity to challenge publicly their own thinking even if it reveals some uncertainty on their part. Leaders need to commit to "we smarter than me" thinking through becoming vulnerable and modeling the suspension of premature judgment.

Administrators would do well to be aware of certain weaknesses inherent in teacher self-assessment. The degree of teacher autonomy or capability to self-assess may vary from teacher to teacher, depending on emotional intelligence, objectivity, self-image, and level of efficacy. Self-interest, lack of time, lack of external evidence, reliance on simplistic explanations, overgeneralization, and inaccurate inferences may hamper accurate self-evaluation (Airasian & Gullickson, 1997).

Portfolio Positives and Problems

One of the most popular forms of teacher self-assessment to emerge in recent years is the portfolio. A *portfolio* is a purposeful collection of materials and artifacts that attempts to demonstrate teacher understanding of subject matter and students and that highlights best teaching practices. A portfolio should include documentation of a teacher's growth over time and reflective statements (Harrington-Leuker, 1996). Portfolios allow teachers to reflect on practice alone with colleagues and can provide examples of accomplished practice that can be adapted into other classrooms (Wolf, 1996). Langer (as cited in Mayo, 1997) suggests these three aspects of a successful portfolio process: (a) collaboration through a study group of trained teachers led by a coach, (b) a broad research-based vision of excellent teaching and learning practice, and (c) teacher compensation or time to participate. Van Wagenen and Hibbard (1998) report that, on the basis of their experiences with portfolios, portfolios have more value when they are more specific and limited in scope and thus tailored to meet the professional development needs of the teacher.

Several drawbacks must be considered in the use of portfolios. In my experience, teachers see them as time-consuming and are reluctant to get involved with them. If portfolios are to be used beneficially, they must be more than a showcase of good-looking pictures and "pretty scrapbook" design. My personal experience with a teacher I hired who presented an outstanding portfolio was that she was ineffective with students and consistently used poor judgment in relating to them. Portfolios need to be considered only a piece of the total picture of a teacher and therefore have limitations for consideration as the best way to go in teacher development and evaluation. Additionally, criteria for what is selected for the portfolio and what purpose it will serve must be made clear. A lack of consensus in what a teacher should know and be able to do makes construction standards difficult, and because it is a personalized document, the lack of standardization makes evaluation difficult (Doolittle, 1994).

Peer Coaching and Peer Evaluation

Peer coaching has been advocated for years, but not until recently has peer evaluation taken the spotlight. This high profile came about, in part, because the National Education Association (NEA) voted in July 1997 to allow creation of peer assistance and review structures through its local affiliates (Chase, 1997). The union vote reversed the NEA's long-standing opposition, and the matter is still highly controversial within the NEA membership ranks. NEA president Bob Chase advocates that professional development of this sort should be at the center of union activities and that, through programs of assistance and review, teachers finally will be taking charge of their profession. Currently, interest in this topic is high in Toledo, Columbus, and Cincinnati, Ohio, as well as in Rochester, New York, and a great deal of work is underway. The School Board of the Cincinnati Public Schools recently approved a peer review process in which teachers evaluate each other (Miller, 1998). The California Legislature recently instituted the first statewide peer review program in the nation (Johnston, 1999). Governor Gray Davis's plan offers incentives for districts to set up peer review and mentoring programs and the withholding of state funds if they do not comply.

The benefits typically shown in the literature are reflected in the next two examples cited. Krovetz and Cohick (1993) report that using *professional development support teams*, a peer coaching program for experienced teachers, in place of a traditional evaluation system had many positive benefits: increased collegiality, reduced isolation, presumed gains from each other's feedback and expertise, and continued support to implement new ideas and so that performance can improve. In the *prime teacher appraisal program*, teachers visit each other's classrooms and make two helpful suggestions and two compliments. Teachers then complete a summative analysis of the 10 compliments and suggestions from the teachers who visited their classrooms at the end of the semester (Allen, Nichols, & LeBlanc, 1997). Teachers receive multiple feedback on their work and are able to gain an appreciation for innovative and diverse approaches used by other teachers. In peer coaching and evaluation, a greater relative expertise is brought to bear by the colleague than is likely by an administrator. The teacher observed will be less able to explain away ineffective methods or curricular choices.

As with any single method, the approach also has disadvantages. Schlechty (1990) points out: "Teachers find it difficult to engage in peer evaluation. . . [S]uch evaluations are too often framed in ways that threaten the delicate patterns of peer support that exist in an organization where peer support is rare" (p. 93). Schrag (1995) notes:

> Teachers are notoriously leery of observing other teachers or permitting colleagues to observe them. The strength of the ethos that classrooms are private sanctuaries clearly deprives teachers of opportunities to see other teachers in action and to receive counsel from colleagues. (p. 644)

Peer coaching and evaluation can also be very time-consuming because they need to take place above and beyond current responsibilities. It is sometimes difficult to arrange time logistically in the everyday school schedule. It requires a lot of trust between the participants and the need for confidentiality. When peer coaching is done by teachers with a previous friendship relationship, it may induce some bias or lack of total honesty. The possibility also exists that peer coaching may damage relationships and create tension among the faculty. Despite these difficulties, I have seen many benefits from peer coaching. I believe that it functions best when it is a teacher-initiated choice for self-evaluation and professional growth.

Other New Approaches

With the push for school and teacher accountability in the political landscape, the focus has been on the relationship between teacher performance and student achievement. Value-added assessment is gaining attention as researchers seek to measure the impact a single teacher can have on student performance. Beginning in the 1998-99 school year in Texas, state law required that teacher evaluation be linked to student performance (Education Week on the Web, 1998). Similarly, Keller (1997) reports that, in Seattle, the new contract calls for a system that fairly ties teacher evaluation to student performance.

Tying teacher evaluation or merit pay to student achievement has produced difficulties in the past, and unless new ways can be found to account for variables, such as inherent student entry differences and the complexity of teaching, we may be doomed to repeat past mistakes. Research has shown that one cannot get dependable data solely from student achievement. Schrag (1995) cautions: "Using student test scores to evaluate teachers necessarily distorts the educational process, and important educational aspirations are pushed out by what are . . . less laudable objectives" (p. 643). In a time when we are more conscious of multiple ways of knowing and the value of developing student dispositions through emotional intelligence, it seems regressive to return to a focus on what can be tested. Achievement results that are used as a compass for reflection and that are a part of several components in an evaluation system are more appropriate than a single high-stakes test to determine an evaluation judgment.

Paying attention to the "customer" is an addition to the Rochester, New York, evaluation system (Lawton, 1997). Parents are asked to fill out a survey that deals with matters of communication between home and school. Rochester is one of the first districts in the country to formalize this option in their teacher contracts. While Rochester was drawing the line at parent-teacher communication and aspects of students' education that are observable by parents, Anchorage, Alaska, was working on a draft form that asked parents to comment on teacher knowledge of content. The Alaska Legislature passed a law requiring multiple feedback sources for teacher evaluation, such as parents, students, colleagues, and community members. Urbanski (1997) cautions that teaching cannot be considered a profession if we go too far: "[A]sking parents whether a teacher knows content or learning styles implies that there is no special knowledge base that teachers have—and that anybody is qualified to assess the specialized knowledge that teachers have" (p. 4).

Manatt (1997) argues for multiple feedback sources in his 360-degree feedback model based on similar practices found in the business world. These sources of feedback are student, peer, parent, principal, student achievement, and self-evaluation. Principals receive all the data in a data set and then apply a rating to the teacher. Principal and teacher then engage in mutual goal setting. Teachers are placed in three tracks, and the majority are able to participate in the 360 track. Even though some aspects to this approach are promising, it also has some problems. The student achievement feedback is based on several years of curriculum work that must be developed and in place. As discussed above, questions remain about the use of student achievement gains as reliable indicators. Student rating effectiveness shows some promise, but instruments need to ask appropriate questions, can be open to mistrust by the student about the teacher's intentions, may not be taken seriously, and may be subject to the popularity versus effectiveness of the teacher being confused. Possibly the biggest obstacles in the 360 system are the facts that teachers are still rated and lack control or choice in the process.

Peterson, Stevens, and Ponzio (1998) favor the use of a variable data source system for several reasons:

■ No single data source is sufficient for all purposes. Excellence in teaching comes in a variety of configurations and areas of performance.

- Good teachers are good for different reasons. The kinds of information that are most helpful in understanding quality vary from one individual teacher to another.

- Not all data are available in one setting.

- The contexts of teaching vary considerably.

Peterson (1995) presents a case for teacher choice in selecting from available data sources because he has evidence to show that teachers are more likely to participate in evaluation when they believe that an accurate picture is being constructed about their teaching. Teacher-controlled systems have important sociological advantages. They are perceived as being fairer to diverse styles and circumstances. Peterson states:

> The task is for teachers to establish their own case for quality performance and credibility in documenting it . . . the systemic change in a teacher-controlled, variable data-evaluation system is a move from the evaluation *of* workers, according to manager expertise, to evaluation done *by* professional teachers. (p. 127)

He also reports valid and reliable comparability of various teachers under this process.

Summary

In terms of combining what we now are learning about all aspects of teaching and learning, it is advantageous to use a variable-data evaluation and professional growth system. My fellow principal colleague Bart DenBoer and I field-tested the evaluation system during the last 4 years. Although developed from our own practice and experiences and independent of any knowledge of Peterson's work, it seems best described, using Peterson's term, as a variable-data system that incorporates the best practices previously described in earlier chapters.

CHAPTER SEVEN

The Growth-Focused
Evaluation System

Why This Name?

First, a few words about the name. Why is this system described as Growth-Focused Evaluation (GFE)? In terms of viewing teachers as professionals and knowledge workers, I believe that the emphasis of the evaluation process for all teachers should be on growth. Growth for the teacher using this system means taking responsibility for his or her own learning and being an active participant in the process. Even though the word *evaluation* can imply something "that is done to" someone in the traditional evaluation mode, I include it in the name of the system to speak to the issue of accountability. Although in this system the principal is ultimately accountable for all teachers, there is a move to a shared accountability.

The Growth-Focused Evaluation System (GFES) notebooks that we distribute to our teachers have five main sections:

1. Introduction and Purpose
2. Professional Growth and Evaluation Process
3. Professional Teaching Practice Domains
4. Teacher Reflection and Practice Instruments
5. Record of Professional Growth

Each of these sections is explained in more detail in succeeding chapters.

The process of development of the GFE system has taken several years. After discussions regarding the current literature and various supervisory approaches, my colleague Bart DenBoer and I decided to give our experienced teachers choices over the types of instruments they would like to use in their evaluation process. After receiving positive teacher response, we began to search out other instruments to use. When the Association for Supervision and Curriculum Development (ASCD) book authored by Charlotte Danielson (1996), *Enhancing Professional Practice: A Framework for Teaching*, arrived in the mail, I thought the missing piece to the puzzle had arrived. Here at last was a meta-analysis of what good teaching was all about and stated in rubric form. Although many previously written documents available listed the qualities of excellent teaching, they lacked the clarity, conciseness, and comprehensive scope of Danielson's work. At last a reference tool was available for working with teachers: We no longer had to argue about the arbitrariness of what constituted good teaching. I immediately called my colleague, and we set to work on a process for teachers that asked them to reflect on their practice by using the standards and self-assessment instruments. Once this was completed, we used the process with our own building teachers, and after reviews by teacher and board committees, the process and system were adopted for use in the Holland (Michigan) Christian Schools beginning with the 1997-98 school year. Since that time, we have presented the model numerous times at workshops and conferences and continue to refine and improve the system as we engage in practice.

The longer we use the GFE system, the more we become convinced of its merit. Contact with each teacher each year enables us to play a more significant role in each individual's growth, as well as in leading staff development in our building. When needed, the process allows us the flexibility to add goals or give direction to teachers in areas that need improvement. While taking the administrative responsibility seriously, in that we maintain control over both "ends" of the process with teacher placement and summative analysis, we believe that the flexibility for teacher choice and direction in the middle truly changes the flavor of the whole experience for teacher and principal. We have seen a higher level of teacher engagement than we ever experienced using clinical supervision. We have seen the development of professional expertise and an increase in collegiality. Furthermore, we are convinced that this process has been an impetus for improved student achievement and individual teacher growth. We have been gratified by the trust received from our teachers after we have extended trust to them and asked them to do work that is meaningful for their context.

The Growth-Focused Evaluation System meets the standard of best practice and current wisdom. Let's examine the GFE system in the light of the factors favoring a new approach listed at the beginning of Chapter 6:

- *Teachers have powerful effects on student learning.* It's where we should focus our energies as administrators if we want to affect student achievement. The GFE system keeps professional growth and evaluation focused on student achievement. It is a continuous process and ties goals and expectations to recognized teacher standards.

- *Teaching is a very complex activity and is not reducible to a set of teaching behaviors.* The GFE system respects the complexity of teaching. The standards used are reflective of both the art and the science aspects of teaching.

- *Supervision and evaluation have several aspects, and the role of principal as sole evaluator has serious limitations.* The principal plays a key role in implementing the system but is generally not asked by the system to function in the typical kinds of traditional situations where his or her effectiveness may be limited. Observation by the principal remains an option for experienced teachers and is required for beginning and marginal teachers in the GFE system.

- *Teachers and principals agree about the ineffectiveness of past supervisory approaches.* The GFE system attempts to approach the supervisory process with honesty and integrity while achieving a high level of results and accountability.

- *Supervisory approaches have shifted from bureaucratic authority to technical authority to a blend of professional and moral authority.* The GFE system encourages continued growth by teachers in professionalism and is a key ingredient in building an environment where moral authority can flourish. One cannot begin to increase professionalism and create a climate of moral authority if evaluation systems are not built on principles of integrity and honesty.

- *The person of the leader is a key ingredient in creating a culture of learning and growth.* What the leader expects is picked up on by the followers. The principal must model practices, such as the GFE system, that have an expectation of continuous growth and improvement, that extend trust, and that seek to engage the teachers fully in the process. The principal plays a key role by example and in designing systems that enhance and encourage teacher growth.

- *We need to find out what motivates teachers to grow; then, we need to design systems that incorporate those principles.* The GFE system relies on intrinsic motivation, rather than on principles of fear and intimidation. Teachers are expected to engage in their own learning and to take responsibility for improvement of their own practice.

- *How we view teachers as professionals and adult learners determines what kinds of structures and processes we set up.* Do we extend trust and expect the best from those we serve and who look to us for leadership? The GFE system expects professional growth from all teachers but differentiates between teacher competencies. It allows flexibility for teachers to meet varying needs within the process.

■ *Structures and processes need to show strong links among supervision and evaluation, professional development, and teaching and learning.* In the GFE system, the linkage among these areas is seamless and interdependent.

The philosophy and content of the GFE system are aligned with the current standards of best practice for teacher evaluation. The GFE system also deals with the following significant issues in a positive manner:

Formative Versus Summative Evaluation. The GFE system recognizes that both formative and summative evaluation are necessary but effectively separates the issue. Whereas in the traditional system the teacher was anxious up to the last word of the evaluation session, the GFE system seeks to remove that anxiety and allows the teacher to focus on the issues of growth and improvement. Under the GFE system, teachers are divided into three tracks: (a) experienced, (b) beginning or transferring, and (c) marginal. The decision to move a teacher into a marginal track would be made in the spring of the year, and the improvement process would begin in the fall. This process is explained further in a later chapter. All teachers know in the fall that their jobs are not in jeopardy unless they do something major during the year to justify a change. This knowledge helps remove the anxiety that builds to the end of a traditional evaluation process and frees teachers to concentrate on growth and improvement during the year.

Building People and a Community of Learners. Continuous self-assessment builds quality into the process, rather than waits to "inspect" at the end. The GFE system is a vehicle for improving relationships between teachers and administrators and for fostering growth. It serves to develop leadership qualities in people and presents a strong model for how schools can focus on learning as our teachers model what we would like our students to be able to do. Both teacher and principal share the burden of learning how to improve job performance. In the GFE system, the teacher takes greater responsibility for his or her own learning, whereas the administrator facilitates and aids the learning done by the teacher through suggestions of resources. The GFE system "gives permission" and direction for teachers to function as colleagues—observing each other, learning from each other, and improving practice together. I have had teachers get into each other's classrooms for the first time in years because it was a choice they made to improve what they were doing. The GFE system honors teachers because it respects them as professionals and values what they bring to students. The GFE system encourages teachers in real-life ways to function as a community of learners.

Essential Questions. Educators are increasingly understanding the value of identifying essential questions about what quality curriculum and instruction should look like. It is equally significant that we develop this habit of reflecting on essential questions about teaching practice with our teachers. At the heart of the GFES evaluation cycle, we ask our teachers to identify questions about their teaching practice and then seek data to explore and answer those questions. Out of that analysis flows an action plan for improvement the following year.

Use of Multiple and Teacher Choice Sources of Data. We believe that, through the use of self-selected questions and instruments for data collection that are linked to standards for practice, we will have flexibility, teacher ownership, and job-embedded, contextual data for our teachers to use. The self-selected questions and instruments will stimulate deep thinking and influence subsequent practice.

Growth-Focused Evaluation System Components

As I mentioned before, when I first began to consider how to change from clinical supervision to some other method of teacher evaluation, I was convinced that I had to put together several components if I wanted to design an effective evaluation and professional growth system. To begin, I knew that it would be unfair to treat all teachers in the same way. As with students, differentiation had to be practiced.

1. *Component 1: Identify teacher types and develop a meaningful and effective process for each.* (This is explained in Chapter 8.) There needed to be an organized, systematic way for principals to communicate with teachers, from an authoritative source, about best practice in teaching. What could I provide teachers that would help them in their reflection about their teaching practice? Was anything out there comprehensive, well organized, research-based, and easily understood?

2. *Component 2: Identify research-based, professional standards to guide teaching practice.* (The source I found is outstanding and has worked very well; it is described in Chapter 9.) What would I ask teachers to do once they were sorted into teacher categories or types? What would be most effective in promoting growth with each type of teacher? How could I engage each teacher on my faculty in continuous improvement through a structure or process? What instruments could be used to help them reflect on their practice? How could they get meaningful feedback to the questions they raised? What should my role be with each type of teacher as their supervisor? Could I develop a system that reflected what I believed and knew to be true from my professional experience?

3. *Component 3: Provide structures, processes, and instruments for teacher reflection and examination of practice.* (These are described in Chapter 10.) What feedback was appropriate for me to share with each teacher? How could I encourage and challenge each as needed? How could I demonstrate accountability for my work with my teachers? What information was helpful for me to know so that I could effectively plan staff development for my school? What information would be helpful for my district to know in planning for staff development?

4. *Component 4: Provide effective feedback for individual and system needs; summarize written records of professional growth and evaluation results.* (Aspects of this component are described in Chapter 11.) How could I design a system that was closely linked to professional development and teaching and learning? Would the teachers see and understand the links among their teaching and learning, professional development, and evaluation? I believed that they would see the link more easily if I included the existing professional growth plan from our district in the GFES notebook. I decided also to ask teachers to maintain their own personal portfolios of selected growth experiences by inserting their goals, evaluation summaries, and principal analyses into a designated section of the notebook.

5. *Component 5: Link the system to the professional development plan for the school district.* (Details about this component are found in Chapter 12.) As mentioned, Chapters 8 through 12 further explain the components of the GFE system and contain practical, how-to descriptions and forms to be used by administrators and teachers. Relevant forms are included in the chapters in reduced form and also appear in order of assembly for a teacher notebook in Resource A, at the end of this book. An administrator in an individual building may copy all forms in the back of the book for use in his or her building only.

TABLE 7.1
Alignment With Theories of Learning and Empowerment

Perkins's Theory One: People learn much of what they have a reasonable opportunity and motivation to learn. Conditions for Theory One to occur:	Covey: Setting up the win-win agreement in empowering workers:	Growth-Focused Evaluation System components:
Clear information Descriptions and examples of the goals and knowledge needed and the performances expected	*Specify desired results* Clarify expectations, set timelines, mutually commit to process *Set guidelines*	*Standards* Framework for Teaching *Examples* (e.g., previous teacher questions) *Process to follow*
Thoughtful practice Opportunity for learners to engage actively and reflectively whatever is to be learned	*Identify available resources* How can they be assisted in getting desired results?	*Selection of instruments for data collection, feedback, and reflection*
Informative feedback Clear, thorough counsel to learners about their performance, helping them proceed more effectively		*Analysis of data collection by teachers* *Conversations with peers and supervisors*
Strong intrinsic or extrinsic motivation Activities that are amply rewarded, either because they are interesting and engaging in themselves or because they feed into other achievements that concern the learner	*Define accountability* *Determine the consequences*	*Selection* of essential question by teacher, *Desire* for personal growth, *System expectations* for accountability, *RISC* (marginal teacher plan)

In summary, I believe that the GFE system incorporates the best in philosophy and practice. As you can see from Table 7.1, the components align with key ideas listed by both Covey (1991) and Perkins (1992).

CHAPTER EIGHT

Identifying Teacher Types

In the Growth-Focused Evaluation (GFE) system, we as administrators provide differentiated supervision through placing teachers in one of three tracks. I agree with Tom McGreal (1993) when he suggests that we "build a system for the 98 percent of teachers who are going to be there for life." From personal experience, I think this makes a lot of sense. In the GFE system, the tracks are (a) experienced teacher, (b) beginning teacher (includes no experience and transferring), and (c) marginal teacher. Most teachers, as McGreal suggests, will be placed in the experienced teacher track. Which track a teacher is placed in will depend mainly on the decision of the principal in consultation with the superintendent and school board (as appropriate). This decision making is very important; it must be handled fairly and courageously with sound evidence for judgment.

How does an administrator encourage growth with a teacher who is resistant to growth and change or downright defiant? I propose a system that I and other administrators in my district are currently using called *required improvement status category (RISC)*. This intermediate step helps ensure that problematic issues are addressed with teachers and that opportunities for change are in place. Although this is possible as an immediate step in non-union schools, I think it has merit for consideration in union contracts. As I have argued previously, teacher quality is such a major variable in improving schools that administrators, unions, and school boards must commit to the improvement of instruction. Having worked in public education in two states as both a teacher and an administrator, I know the frustrations of excellent teachers and administrators regarding the union protectionism that sometimes exists. When ineffective teachers are protected and the focus becomes legal rights rather than the rights of children and parents to quality instruction, the effects on the morale of all in education are devastating. The step of RISC is designed to be preventive; it is similar to getting help for failing students before they get bad enough to "qualify" for formal assistance. Why should we wait to deal with small, nagging problems we see in teacher performance and attitude? Why wait until those problems become so entrenched and so large that we must consider probation or termination? Isn't an intermediary step both more humane to the teacher and beneficial to the students whose learning the teacher is responsible for? I suggest that teacher unions, school boards, and administrators take a more proactive approach toward working in the best interests of teachers, students, and parents by considering inclusion of this concept.

In Chapter 10, I describe in more detail the GFE system for each of the three teacher types. For the purposes of the GFE system, then, teachers are sorted into three categories:

1. *Experienced:* 3 or more years of successful teaching experience

2. *Beginning:* New teacher, 2 or fewer years of teaching experience; transferring, 2 years or fewer in a new situation

3. *Marginal:* Experienced teacher who needs to make improvements in one or more areas (this category is further described in Chapter 10)

When using this system for the first time, principals must determine which category is applicable for each teacher. This decision should be made in consultation with the superintendent and other appropriate members of the administrative team in a district.

How can we determine which teachers to place in which tracks? Obviously, we know who our beginning or transferring teachers are, so that assignment is rather easy. How do we decide who qualifies as experienced and who is designated as marginal in some way? Actually, determining less than acceptable teaching performance is not a task administrators struggle with a great deal (see Brandt, 1996; Schrag, 1995). Peterson et al. (1998) report that, in using teacher-chosen variable data sources, "truly bad teachers have great difficulty producing any favorable results . . . [B]ad teachers are readily identified by administrator monitoring" (p. 129). I know this to be true from personal experience as well. Administrators have daily contact with teachers, parents, and students and hear various forms of feedback, as they circulate through classrooms and the school, that lead to informed opinions. "Managing by wandering around" is reported as a technique that, when properly done, helps principals stay informed and is an important way to facilitate reflective practice among teachers (Reitzug & Burrello, 1995).

What we know as leaders at a gut level, our intuition, is now being validated through science. Intuitive astuteness may be a skill that all humans share and that managers have developed to an even greater degree. Goleman (1998) reports on studies done at Harvard:

> People can sense intuitively in the first thirty seconds of an encounter what basic impression they will have of the other person after fifteen minutes—or half a year. For instance, when people watch just thirty-second snatches of teachers giving a lecture, they can assess each teacher's proficiency with about 80 percent accuracy. (p. 53)

These data are based on 45 studies done by Ambady and Rosenthal. This kind of intuitive astuteness happens as the result of many accumulated previous experiences, which enable the observer to read a new situation quickly.

Principals will make better decisions about teacher types if they are actively involved in the life of the school. They must get into classrooms for a variety of reasons. They need to be able to say to parents: "I know what is going on in that classroom because I have been in there many times." They must be in touch with parents and students—the "customers." It is important that effective communication occur on a regular basis between school and parents and that principals understand how the teacher is communicating to parents. Establishing an open, trusting environment where suggestions and comments are received and listened to are vital elements for getting reliable feedback from parents, teachers, and students. As administrators, we must model the desire for feedback and remind our teachers that high performers are always interested in, and seek out, feedback.

In the case of beginning or transferring teachers, the main concern is that the teachers be effective in their new environment. Principals must regularly spend time in the rooms on both an informal and a formal basis. We must ensure that quality instruction is happening and that it meets the acceptable level as described in the standards in the framework. I see value in using the clinical supervision model for these teachers. I also recommend assigning a mentor teacher to the new or transferring teacher. Although other, more meaningful peer relationships may supersede the mentor relationship, it is still a crucial piece to put in place so that teacher assistance occurs on a systematic basis.

Blanchard, Zigarmi, and Zigarmi's book *Leadership and the One Minute Manager* (1985) has been helpful to me in terms of thinking about matching leadership style to developmental level. As I thought about teacher types, they fell nicely into Table 8.1, which I adapted from Blanchard et al.'s book.

Before we get into the evaluation and professional growth process for each teacher type, we need to look at what teaching standards will be able to help us in our conversations with teachers and as a tool for teachers to consider their professional practice against.

TABLE 8.1

Identifying Teacher Types Using Blanchard's Developmental Levels

Developmental Level— Blanchard	Appropriate Leadership Style—Blanchard	Teacher Type
Low competence High commitment	Directing Structure, control, supervise	Beginning
Some competence Low commitment	Coaching Direct and support	Marginal
High competence Variable commitment	Supporting Praise, listen, facilitate	Experienced Effective
High competence High commitment	Delegating Turn over responsibility for day-to-day decision making	Experienced Highly effective Mentors

SOURCE: Data in columns 1 and 2 are from *Leadership and the One Minute Manager*, by K. Blanchard, P. Zigarmi, and D. Zigarmi, 1985, New York: Morrow. Reprinted by permission.

CHAPTER NINE

The Need for Standards

Put a group of educators together in a room and ask them what excellent teaching is. Although the discussion will generate many significant ideas about what constitutes good teaching, there may not be total agreement. This lack of agreement has been a difficulty in principal-teacher conversations about teaching. They have no common reference point of agreement. What one person values may not be as valued by another, and debates about what is more important can ensue. Both teacher and administrator judgments may be arbitrary or idiosyncratic. Airasian and Gullickson (1997) report, "There is an absence of well-defined standards and criteria for teacher self-evaluation, just as there is for teacher evaluation in general" (p. 12). Giving the benefit of the doubt to those fine authors, however, those words may have been written before the authors were aware of the outstanding compilation of professional teaching practices— *Enhancing Professional Practice: A Framework for Teaching*, by Charlotte Danielson (1996). This book is a well-organized and comprehensive means to "get a handle on" the complexity of teaching, reflecting the results of extensive research on teaching over the years. The document is divided into four main teaching domains and 22 components, with each component laid out in rubric form. It is an excellent resource that can be used with experienced, beginning, or marginal teachers. The features and assumptions of the framework are summarized below (from Danielson, pp. 21, 28):

Features of the Framework

- Comprehensive

- Not a checklist of teaching behaviors

- Not an endorsement of a particular teaching style or organizational structure

- Dependent on context

- Can be demonstrated in diverse ways

Assumptions of the Framework

- Derives from research

- Reflects a new paradigm for learning and teaching that is grounded in the constructivist approach to teaching

- Focuses on the purposeful nature of teaching

- Creates a community of learners

- Recognizes the role of appropriateness in making decisions

- Asserts that teaching is a profession

The framework serves as an invaluable guide for teacher conversation in the Growth-Focused Evaluation (GFE) system. It incorporates empirical research on teaching practice into one easy-to-use document. The framework includes four main components of professional teaching practice:

1. Planning and Preparation
2. The Classroom Environment
3. Instruction
4. Professional Responsibilities

In the GFE system, experienced teachers are instructed to use the framework in Years 1 or 2 to help them reflect on their instructional practice and to set appropriate professional growth goals. During the evaluation year (Year 3), teachers usually select a goal from Domain 3—Instruction. They must formulate a question or questions about their instructional practices related to one of the components listed under the Domain Instruction (this process is described in greater detail in Chapter 10). Beginning teachers can use the framework as a reference tool to identify areas they need to strengthen next. Because the framework describes each domain in rubric format, teachers can see what the next level of proficiency they are aspiring to will look like. The rubrics give a common language for administrators and teachers to use in identifying and discussing problems with marginal teachers. As Danielson states, the framework can be a road map for the novice teacher and provide guidance and a common language for the experienced professional; it is helpful for all teacher types.

NOTE: Charlotte Danielson has graciously granted permission for the domain charts to be reproduced in this chapter for purposes of demonstrating how the framework is used in the context of the GFE system. I express deep appreciation to her for this privilege. It is *highly recommended* that you purchase her book. A valuable rationale, explanation, and documentation section accompanies each domain chart, as well as excellent suggestions on how the book can be used for a variety of purposes. The book can be purchased from the Association for Supervision and Curriculum Development (ASCD), 1703 North Beauregard Street, Alexandria, VA 22311-1714 or www.ascd.org.

An overview of the framework follows (Figure 9.1), and then the summary rubrics for each of the four teaching domains (Figures 9.2 through 9.5). They are included here so that the reader can become familiar with them. No further copying may be done without permission.

DOMAIN 1: PLANNING AND PREPARATION

Component 1a: Demonstrating Knowledge of Content and Pedagogy
- Knowledge of content
- Knowledge of prerequisite relationships
- Knowledge of content-related pedagogy

Component 1b: Demonstrating Knowledge of Students
- Knowledge of characteristics of age-group
- Knowledge of students' varied approaches to learning
- Knowledge of students' skills and knowledge
- Knowledge of students' interests and cultural heritage

Component 1c: Selecting Instructional Goals
- Value
- Clarity
- Suitability for diverse students
- Balance

Component 1d: Demonstrating Knowledge of Resources
- Resources for teaching
- Resources for students

Component 1e: Designing Coherent Instruction
- Learning activities
- Instructional materials and resources
- Instructional groups
- Lesson and unit structure

Component 1f: Assessing Student Learning
- Congruence with instructional goals
- Criteria and standards
- Use for planning

DOMAIN 2: THE CLASSROOM ENVIRONMENT

Component 2a: Creating an Environment of Respect and Rapport
- Teacher interaction with students
- Student interaction

Component 2b: Establishing a Culture for Learning
- Importance of the content
- Student pride in work
- Expectations for learning and achievement

Component 2c: Managing Classroom Procedures
- Management of instructional groups
- Management of transitions
- Management of materials and supplies
- Performance of non-instructional duties
- Supervision of volunteers and paraprofessionals

Component 2d: Managing Student Behavior
- Expectations
- Monitoring of student behavior
- Response to student misbehavior

Component 2e: Organizing Physical Space
- Safety and arrangement of furniture
- Accessibility to learning and use of physical resources

Figure 9.1.
Overview of Professional Teaching Practice Domains:
Components of Professional Practice

DOMAIN 3: INSTRUCTION

Component 3a: Communicating Clearly and Accurately
- Directions and procedures
- Oral and written language

Component 3b: Using Questioning and Discussion Techniques
- Quality of questions
- Discussion techniques
- Student participation

Component 3c: Engaging Students in Learning
- Representation of content
- Activities and assignments
- Grouping of students
- Instructional materials and resources
- Structure and pacing

Component 3d: Providing Feedback to Students
- Quality: accurate, substantive, constructive, and specific
- Timeliness

Component 3e: Demonstrating Flexibility and Responsiveness
- Lesson adjustment
- Response to students
- Persistence

DOMAIN 4: PROFESSIONAL RESPONSIBILITIES

Component 4a: Reflecting on Teaching
- Accuracy
- Use in future teaching

Component 4b: Maintaining Accurate Records
- Student completion of assignments
- Student progress in learning
- Non-instructional records

Component 4c: Communicating With Families
- Information about the instructional program
- Information about individual students
- Engagement of families in the instructional program

Component 4d: Contributing to the School and District
- Relationships with colleagues
- Service to the school
- Participation in school and district projects

Component 4e: Growing and Developing Professionally
- Enhancement of content knowledge and pedagogical skill
- Service to the profession

Component 4f: Showing Professionalism
- Service to students
- Advocacy
- Decision making

Figure 9.1.
Continued

DOMAIN 1: PLANNING AND PREPARATION
Component 1a: Demonstrating Knowledge of Content and Pedagogy
Elements: Knowledge of content ● Knowledge of prerequisite relationships ● Knowledge of content-related pedagogy

LEVEL OF PERFORMANCE

ELEMENT	UNSATISFACTORY	BASIC	PROFICIENT	DISTINGUISHED
Knowledge of Content	Teacher makes content errors or does not correct content errors students make.	Teacher displays basic content knowledge but cannot articulate connections with other parts of the discipline or with other disciplines.	Teacher displays solid content knowledge and makes connections between the content and other parts of the discipline and other disciplines.	Teacher displays extensive content knowledge with evidence of continuing pursuit of such knowledge.
Knowledge of Prerequisite Relationships	Teacher displays little understanding of prerequisite knowledge important for student learning of the content.	Teacher indicates some awareness of prerequisite learning, although such knowledge may be incomplete or inaccurate.	Teacher's plans and practices reflect understanding of prerequisite relationships among topics and concepts.	Teacher actively builds on knowledge of prerequisite relationships when describing instruction or seeking causes for student misunderstanding.
Knowledge of Content-Related Pedagogy	Teacher displays little understanding of pedagogical issues involved in student learning of the content.	Teacher displays basic pedagogical knowledge but does not anticipate student misconceptions.	Pedagogical practices reflect current research on best pedagogical practice within the discipline but without anticipating student misconceptions.	Teacher displays continuing search for best practice and anticipates student misconceptions.

DOMAIN 1: PLANNING AND PREPARATION
Component 1b: Demonstrating Knowledge of Students
Elements: Knowledge of characteristics (intellectual, social, and emotional) of age group ● Knowledge of students' varied approaches to learning ● Knowledge of students' skills and knowledge ● Knowledge of students' interests and cultural heritage

LEVEL OF PERFORMANCE

ELEMENT	UNSATISFACTORY	BASIC	PROFICIENT	DISTINGUISHED
Knowledge of Characteristics of Age Group	Teacher displays minimal knowledge of developmental characteristics of age group.	Teacher displays generally accurate knowledge of developmental characteristics of age group.	Teacher displays thorough understanding of typical developmental characteristics of age group, as well as exceptions to general patterns.	Teacher displays knowledge of typical developmental characteristics of age group, exceptions to the patterns, and the extent to which each student follows patterns.
Knowledge of Students' Varied Approaches to Learning	Teacher is unfamiliar with the different approaches to learning that students exhibit, such as learning styles, modalities, and different "intelligences."	Teacher displays general understanding of the different approaches to learning that students exhibit.	Teacher displays solid understanding of the different approaches to learning that different students exhibit.	Teacher uses, where appropriate, knowledge of students' varied approaches to learning in instructional planning.
Knowledge of Students' Skills and Knowledge	Teacher displays little knowledge of students' skills and knowledge and does not indicate that such knowledge is valuable.	Teacher recognizes the value of understanding students' skills and knowledge but displays this knowledge for the class only as a whole.	Teacher displays knowledge of students' skills and knowledge for groups of students and recognizes the value of this knowledge.	Teacher displays knowledge of students' skills and knowledge for each student, including those with special needs.
Knowledge of Students' Interests and Cultural Heritage	Teacher displays little understanding of students' interests or cultural heritage and does not indicate that such knowledge is valuable.	Teacher recognizes the value of understanding students' interests or cultural heritage but displays this knowledge for the class only as a whole.	Teacher displays knowledge of the interests or cultural heritage of groups of students and recognizes the value of this knowledge.	Teacher displays knowledge of the interests or cultural heritage of each student.

Figure 9.2.
Summary Rubric for Domain 1

DOMAIN 1: PLANNING AND PREPARATION
Component 1c: Selecting Instructional Goals

Elements: VALUE: Goals represent high expectations for students; and reflect important learning and conceptual understanding, curriculum standards, and frameworks ● CLARITY: Goals are clearly stated as student learning and permit sound assessment ● SUITABILITY FOR DIVERSE STUDENTS: Goals reflect needs of all students in a class ● BALANCE: Goals represent opportunities for the different types of learning—for example, thinking as well as knowledge—and coordination or integration within or across disciplines

LEVEL OF PERFORMANCE

ELEMENT	UNSATISFACTORY	BASIC	PROFICIENT	DISTINGUISHED
Value	Goals are not valuable and represent low expectations or no conceptual understanding for students.	Goals do not reflect important learning.	Goals are moderately valuable in either their expectations or conceptual understanding for students and in importance of learning.	Goals are valuable in their level of expectations, conceptual understanding, and importance of learning.
Clarity	Goals are either not clear or are stated as student activities. Goals do not permit viable methods of assessment.	Goals are only moderately clear or include a combination of goals and activities. Some goals do not permit viable methods of assessment.	Most of the goals are clear but may include a few activities. Most permit viable methods of assessment.	All the goals are clear, written in the form of student learning, and permit viable methods of assessment.
Suitability for Diverse Students	Goals are not suitable for the class.	Most of the goals are suitable for most students in the class.	All the goals are suitable for most students in the class.	Goals take into account the varying learning needs of individual students or groups.
Balance	Goals reflect only one type of learning and one discipline or strand.	Goals reflect several types of learning but no effort at coordination or integration.	Goals reflect several different types of learning and opportunities for integration.	Goals reflect student initiative in establishing important learning.

DOMAIN 1: PLANNING AND PREPARATION
Component 1d: Demonstrating Knowledge of Resources

Elements: Resources for teaching ● Resources for students

LEVEL OF PERFORMANCE

ELEMENT	UNSATISFACTORY	BASIC	PROFICIENT	DISTINGUISHED
Resources for Teaching	Teacher is unaware of resources available through the school or district.	Teacher displays limited awareness of resources available through the school or district.	Teacher is fully aware of all resources available through the school or district.	In addition to being aware of school and district resources, teacher actively seeks other materials to enhance instruction—for example, from professional organizations or through the community.
Resources for Students	Teacher is unaware of resources available to assist students who need them.	Teacher displays limited awareness of resources available through the school or district.	Teacher is fully aware of all resources available through the school or district and knows how to gain access for students.	In addition to being aware of school and district resources, teacher is aware of additional resources available through the community.

Figure 9.2.
Continued

DOMAIN 1: PLANNING AND PREPARATION
Component 1e: Designing Coherent Instruction
Elements: Learning Activities ● Instructional materials and resources ● Instructional groups ● Lesson and unit structure

LEVEL OF PERFORMANCE

ELEMENT	UNSATISFACTORY	BASIC	PROFICIENT	DISTINGUISHED
Learning Activities	Learning activities are not suitable to students or instructional goals. They do not follow an organized progression and do not reflect recent professional research.	Only some of the learning activities are suitable to students or instructional goals. Progression of activities in the unit is uneven, and only some activities reflect recent professional research.	Most of the learning activities are suitable to students and instructional goals. Progression of activities in the unit is fairly even, and most activities reflect recent professional research.	Learning activities are highly relevant to students and instructional goals. They progress coherently, producing a unified whole and reflecting recent professional research.
Instructional Materials and Resources	Materials and resources do not support the instructional goals or engage students in meaningful learning.	Some of the materials and resources support the instructional goals, and some engage students in meaningful learning.	All materials and resources support the instructional goals, and most engage students in meaningful learning.	All materials and resources support the instructional goals, and most engage students in meaningful learning. There is evidence of student participation in selecting or adapting materials.
Instructional Groups	Instructional groups do not support the instructional goals and offer no variety.	Instructional groups are inconsistent in suitability to the instructional goals and offer minimal variety.	Instructional groups are varied, as appropriate to the different instructional goals.	Instructional groups are varied, as appropriate to the different instructional groups. There is evidence of student choice in selecting different patterns of instructional groups.
Lesson and Unit Structure	The lesson or unit has no clearly defined structure, or the structure is chaotic. Time allocations are unrealistic.	The lesson or unit has a recognizable structure, although the structure is not uniformly maintained throughout. Most time allocations are reasonable.	The lesson or unit has a clearly defined structure that activities are organized around. Time allocations are reasonable.	The lesson's or unit's structure is clear and allows for different pathways according to student needs.

DOMAIN 1: PLANNING AND PREPARATION
Component 1f: Assessing Student Learning
Elements: Congruence with instructional goals ● Criteria and standards ● Use for planning

LEVEL OF PERFORMANCE

ELEMENT	UNSATISFACTORY	BASIC	PROFICIENT	DISTINGUISHED
Congruence With Instructional Goals	Content and methods of assessment lack congruence with instructional goals.	Some of the instructional goals are assessed through the proposed approach, but many are not.	All the instructional goals are nominally assessed through the proposed plan, but the approach is more suitable to some goals than to others.	The proposed approach to assessment is completely congruent with the instructional goals, both in content and process.
Criteria and Standards	The proposed approach contains no clear criteria or standards.	Assessment criteria and standards have been developed, but they are either not clear or have not been clearly communicated to students.	Assessment criteria and standards are clear and have been clearly communicated to students.	Assessment criteria and standards are clear and have been clearly communicated to students. There is evidence that students contributed to the development of the criteria and standards.
Use for Planning	The assessment results affect planning for these students only minimally.	Teacher uses assessment results to plan for the class as a whole.	Teacher uses assessment results to plan for individuals and groups of students.	Students are aware of how they are meeting the established standards and participate in planning the next steps.

Figure 9.2.
Continued

DOMAIN 2: THE CLASSROOM ENVIRONMENT
Component 2a: Creating an Environment of Respect and Rapport
Elements: Teacher interaction with students ● Student interaction

LEVEL OF PERFORMANCE

ELEMENT	UNSATISFACTORY	BASIC	PROFICIENT	DISTINGUISHED
Teacher Interaction With Students	Teacher interaction with at least some students is negative, demeaning, sarcastic, or inappropriate to the age or culture of the students. Students exhibit disrespect.	Teacher-student interactions are generally appropriate but may reflect occasional inconsistencies, favoritism, or disregard for students' cultures. Students exhibit only minimal respect for teacher.	Teacher-student interactions are friendly and demonstrate general warmth, caring, and respect. Such interactions are appropriate to developmental and cultural norms. Students exhibit respect for teacher.	Teacher demonstrates genuine caring and respect for individual students. Students exhibit respect for teacher as an individual, beyond that for the role.
Student Interaction	Student interactions are characterized by conflict, sarcasm, or put-downs.	Students do not demonstrate negative behavior toward one another.	Student interactions are generally polite and respectful.	Students demonstrate genuine caring for one another as individuals and as students.

DOMAIN 2: THE CLASSROOM ENVIRONMENT
Component 2b: Establishing a Culture for Learning
Elements: Importance of the content ● Student pride in work ● Expectations for learning and achievement

LEVEL OF PERFORMANCE

ELEMENT	UNSATISFACTORY	BASIC	PROFICIENT	DISTINGUISHED
Importance of the Content	Teacher or students convey a negative attitude toward the content, suggesting that the content is not important or is mandated by others.	Teacher communicates importance of the work but with little conviction and only minimal apparent buy-in by the students.	Teacher conveys genuine enthusiasm for the subject, and students demonstrate consistent commitment to its value.	Students demonstrate through their active participation, curiosity, and attention to detail that they value the content's importance.
Student Pride in Work	Students demonstrate little or no pride in their work. They seem to be motivated by the desire to complete a task rather than do high-quality work.	Students minimally accept the responsibility to "do good work" but invest little of their energy in the quality of the work	Students accept teacher insistence on work of high quality and demonstrate pride in that work.	Students take obvious pride in their work and initiate improvements in it—for example, by revising drafts on their own initiative, helping peers, and ensuring that high-quality work is displayed.
Expectations for Learning and Achievement	Instructional goals and activities, interactions, and the classroom environment convey only modest expectations for student achievement.	Instructional goals and activities, interactions, and the classroom environment convey inconsistent expectations for student achievement.	Instructional goals and activities, interactions, and the classroom environment convey high expectations for student achievement.	Both students and teacher establish and maintain through planning of learning activities, interactions, and the classroom environment high expectations for the learning of all students.

Figure 9.3.
Summary Rubric for Domain 2

DOMAIN 2: THE CLASSROOM ENVIRONMENT
Component 2c: Managing Classroom Procedures
Elements: Management of instructional groups ● Management of transitions ● Management of materials and supplies
● Performance of non-instructional duties ● Supervision of volunteers and paraprofessionals

LEVEL OF PERFORMANCE

ELEMENT	UNSATISFACTORY	BASIC	PROFICIENT	DISTINGUISHED
Management of Instructional Groups	Students not working with the teacher are not productively engaged in learning.	Tasks for group work are partially organized, resulting in some off-task behavior when teacher is involved with one group.	Tasks for group work are organized, and groups are managed so that most students are engaged at all times.	Groups working independently are productively engaged at all times, with students assuming responsibility for productivity.
Management of Transitions	Much time is lost during transitions.	Transitions are sporadically efficient, resulting in some loss of instructional time.	Transitions occur smoothly, with little loss of instructional time.	Transitions are seamless, with students assuming some responsibility for efficient operation.
Management of Materials and Supplies	Materials are handled inefficiently, resulting in loss of instructional time.	Routines for handling materials and supplies function moderately well.	Routines for handling materials and supplies occur smoothly, with little loss of instructional time.	Routines for handling materials and supplies are seamless, with students assuming some responsibility for efficient operation.
Performance of Non-Instructional Duties	Considerable instructional time is lost in performing non-instructional duties.	Systems for performing non-instructional duties are fairly efficient, resulting in little loss of instructional time.	Efficient systems for performing non-instructional duties are in place, resulting in minimal loss of instructional time.	Systems for performing non-instructional duties are well established, with students assuming considerable responsibility for efficient operation.
Supervision of Volunteers and Paraprofessionals	Volunteers and paraprofessionals have no clearly defined duties or do nothing most of the time.	Volunteers and para-professionals are productively engaged during the portions of class time but require frequent supervision.	Volunteers and para-professionals productively are independently engaged during the entire class.	Volunteers and paraprofes-sionals make a substantive contribution to the classroom environment.

Figure 9.3.
Continued

DOMAIN 2: THE CLASSROOM ENVIRONMENT
Component 2d: Managing Student Behavior
Elements: Expectations • Monitoring of student behavior • Response to student misbehavior

LEVEL OF PERFORMANCE

ELEMENT	UNSATISFACTORY	BASIC	PROFICIENT	DISTINGUISHED
Expectations	No standards of conduct appear to have been established, or students are confused as to what the standards are.	Standards of conduct appear to have been established for most situations, and most students seem to understand them.	Standards of conduct are clear to all students.	Standards of conduct are clear to all students and appear to have been developed with student participation.
Monitoring of Student Behavior	Student behavior is not monitored, and teacher is unaware of what students are doing.	Teacher is generally aware of student behavior but may miss the activities of some students.	Teacher is alert to student behavior at all times.	Monitoring by teacher is subtle and preventive. Students monitor their own and their peers' behavior, correcting one another respectfully.
Response to Student Misbehavior	Teacher does not respond to misbehavior, or the response is inconsistent, overly repressive, or does not respect the student's dignity.	Teacher attempts to respond to student misbehavior but with uneven results, or no serious disruptive behavior occurs.	Teacher response to misbehavior is appropriate and successful and respects the student's dignity, or student behavior is generally appropriate.	Teacher response to misbehavior is highly effective and sensitive to students' individual needs, or student behavior is entirely appropriate.

DOMAIN 2: THE CLASSROOM ENVIRONMENT
Component 2e: Organizing Physical Space
Elements: Safety and arrangement of furniture • Accessibility to learning and use of physical resources

LEVEL OF PERFORMANCE

ELEMENT	UNSATISFACTORY	BASIC	PROFICIENT	DISTINGUISHED
Safety and Arrangement of Furniture	The classroom is unsafe, or the furniture arrangement is not suited to the lesson activities, or both.	The classroom is safe, and classroom furniture is adjusted for a lesson, or if necessary, a lesson is adjusted to the furniture, but with limited effectiveness.	The classroom is safe, and the furniture arrangement is a resource for learning activities.	The classroom is safe, and students adjust the furniture to advance their own purposes in learning.
Accessibility to Learning and Use of Physical Resources	Teacher uses physical resources poorly, or learning is not accessible to some students.	Teacher uses physical resources adequately, and at least essential learning is accessible to all students.	Teacher uses physical resources skillfully, and all learning is equally accessible to all students.	Both teacher and students use physical resources optimally, and students ensure that all learning is equally accessible to all students.

Figure 9.3.
Continued

DOMAIN 3: INSTRUCTION
Component 3a: Communicating Clearly and Accurately
Elements: Directions and procedures ● Oral and written language

LEVEL OF PERFORMANCE

ELEMENT	UNSATISFACTORY	BASIC	PROFICIENT	DISTINGUISHED
Directions and Procedures	Teacher directions and procedures are confusing to students.	Teacher directions and procedures are clarified after initial student confusion or are excessively detailed.	Teacher directions and procedures are clear to students and contain an appropriate level of detail.	Teacher directions and procedures are clear to students and anticipate possible student misunderstanding.
Oral and Written Language	Teacher's spoken language is inaudible, or written language is illegible. Spoken or written language may contain many grammar and syntax errors. Vocabulary may be inappropriate, vague, or used incorrectly, leaving students confused.	Teacher's spoken language is audible, and written language is legible. Both are used correctly. Vocabulary is correct but limited or is not appropriate to students' ages or backgrounds.	Teacher's spoken and written language is clear and correct. Vocabulary is appropriate to students' age and interests.	Teacher's spoken and written language is correct and expressive, with well-chosen vocabulary that enriches the lesson.

DOMAIN 3: INSTRUCTION
Component 3b: Using Questioning and Discussion Techniques
Elements: Quality of questions ● Discussion techniques ● Student participation

LEVEL OF PERFORMANCE

ELEMENT	UNSATISFACTORY	BASIC	PROFICIENT	DISTINGUISHED
Quality of Questions	Teacher's questions are virtually all of poor quality.	Teacher's questions are a combination of low and high quality. Only some invite a response.	Most of teacher's questions are of high quality. Adequate time is available for students to respond.	Teacher's questions are of uniformly high quality, with adequate time for students to respond. Students formulate many questions.
Discussion Techniques	Interaction between teacher and students is predominantly recitation style, with teacher mediating all questions and answers.	Teacher makes some attempt to engage students in a true discussion, with uneven results.	Classroom interaction represents true discussion, with teacher stepping, when appropriate, to the side.	Students assume considerable responsibility for the success of the discussion, initiating topics and making unsolicited contributions.
Student Participation	Only a few students participate in the discussion.	Teacher attempts to engage all students in the discussion, but with only limited success.	Teacher successfully engages all students in the discussion.	Students themselves ensure that all voices are heard in the discussion.

Figure 9.4.
Summary Rubric for Domain 3

DOMAIN 3: INSTRUCTION
Component 3c: Engaging Students in Learning
Elements: Representation of content ● Activities and assignments ● Grouping of students
● Instructional materials and resources ● Structure and pacing

LEVEL OF PERFORMANCE

ELEMENT	UNSATISFACTORY	BASIC	PROFICIENT	DISTINGUISHED
Representation of Content	Representation of content is inappropriate and unclear or uses poor examples and analogies.	Representation of content is inconsistent in quality: some is done skillfully, with good examples; other portions are difficult to follow.	Representation of content is appropriate and links well with students' knowledge and experience.	Representation of content is appropriate and links well with students' knowledge and experience. Students contribute to representation of content.
Activities and Assignments	Activities and assignments are inappropriate for students in terms of their age or background. Students are not engaged mentally.	Some activities and assignments are appropriate to students and engage them mentally, but others do not.	Most activities and assignments are appropriate to students. Almost all students are cognitively engaged in them.	All students are cognitively engaged in the activities and assignments in their exploration of content. Students initiate or adapt activities and projects to enhance understanding.
Grouping of Students	Instructional groups are inappropriate to the students or to the instructional goals.	Instructional groups are only partially appropriate to the students or only moderately successful in advancing the instructional goals of a lesson.	Instructional groups are productive and fully appropriate to the students or to the instructional goals of a lesson.	Instructional groups are productive and fully appropriate to the instructional goals of a lesson. Students take the initiative to influence instructional groups to advance their understanding.
Instructional Materials and Resources	Instructional materials and resources are unsuitable to the instructional goals or do not engage students mentally.	Instructional materials and resources are partially suitable to the instructional goals, or students' level of mental engagement is moderate.	Instructional materials and resources are suitable to the instructional goals and engage students mentally.	Instructional materials and resources are suitable to the instructional goals and engage students mentally. Students initiate the choice, adaptation, or creation of materials to enhance their own purposes.
Structure and Pacing	The lesson has no clearly defined structure, or the pacing of the lesson is too slow or rushed, or both.	The lesson has a recognizable structure, although it is not uniformly maintained throughout the lesson. Pacing of the lesson is inconsistent.	The lesson has a clearly defined structure around which the activities are organized. Pacing of the lesson is consistent.	The lesson's structure is highly coherent, allowing for reflection and closure as appropriate. Pacing of the lesson is appropriate for all students.

Figure 9.4.
Continued

DOMAIN 3: INSTRUCTION
Component 3d: Providing Feedback to Students
Elements: Quality: accurate, substantive, constructive, and specific ● Timeliness

LEVEL OF PERFORMANCE

ELEMENT	UNSATISFACTORY	BASIC	PROFICIENT	DISTINGUISHED
Quality: Accurate, Substantive, Constructive, and Specific	Feedback is either not provided or is of uniformly poor quality.	Feedback is inconsistent in quality: Some elements of high quality are present; others are not.	Feedback is consistently high quality.	Feedback is consistently high quality. Provision is made for students to use feedback in their learning.
Timeliness	Feedback is not provided in a timely manner.	Timeliness of feedback is inconsistent.	Feedback is consistently provided in a timely manner.	Feedback is consistently provided in a timely manner. Students make prompt use of the feedback in their learning.

DOMAIN 3: INSTRUCTION
Component 3e: Demonstrating Flexibility and Responsiveness
Elements: Lesson adjustment ● Response to students ● Persistence

LEVEL OF PERFORMANCE

ELEMENT	UNSATISFACTORY	BASIC	PROFICIENT	DISTINGUISHED
Lesson Adjustment	Teacher adheres rigidly to an instructional plan even when a change will clearly improve a lesson.	Teacher attempts to adjust a lesson, with mixed results.	Teacher makes a minor adjustment to a lesson, and the adjustment occurs smoothly.	Teacher successfully makes a major adjustment to a lesson.
Response to Students	Teacher ignores or brushes aside students' questions or interests.	Teacher attempts to accommodate students' questions or interests. The effects on the coherence of a lesson are uneven.	Teacher successfully accommodates students' questions or interests.	Teacher seizes a major opportunity to enhance learning, building on a spontaneous event.
Persistence	When a student has difficulty learning, the teacher either gives up or blames the student or the environment for the student's lack of success.	Teacher accepts responsibility for the success of all students but has only a limited repertoire of instructional strategies to use.	Teacher persists in seeking approaches for students who have difficulty learning, possessing a moderate repertoire of strategies.	Teacher persists in seeking effective approaches for students who need help, using an extensive repertoire of strategies and soliciting additional resources from the school.

Figure 9.4.
Continued

DOMAIN 4: PROFESSIONAL RESPONSIBILITIES
Component 4a: Reflecting on Teaching
Elements: Accuracy ● Use in future teaching

LEVEL OF PERFORMANCE

ELEMENT	UNSATISFACTORY	BASIC	PROFICIENT	DISTINGUISHED
Accuracy	Teacher does not know if a lesson was effective or achieved its goals, or profoundly misjudges the success of a lesson.	Teacher has a general accurate impression of a lesson's effectiveness and the extent to which instructional goals were met.	Teacher makes an accurate assessment of a lesson's effectiveness and the extent to which it achieved its goals and can cite general references to support the judgment.	Teacher makes a thoughtful and accurate assessment of a lesson's effectiveness and the extent to which it achieved its goals, citing many specific examples from the lesson and weighing the relative strength of each.
Use in Future Teaching	Teacher has no suggestions for how a lesson may be improved another time.	Teacher makes general suggestions about how a lesson may be improved.	Teacher makes a few specific suggestions of what he or she may try another time.	Drawing on an extensive repertoire of skills, the teacher offers specific alternative actions, complete with probable successes of different approaches.

DOMAIN 4: PROFESSIONAL RESPONSIBILITIES
Component 4b: Maintaining Accurate Records
Elements: Student completion of assignments ● Student progress in learning ● Non-instructional records

LEVEL OF PERFORMANCE

ELEMENT	UNSATISFACTORY	BASIC	PROFICIENT	DISTINGUISHED
Student Completion of Assignments	Teacher's system for maintaining information on student completion of assignments is in disarray.	Teacher's system for maintaining information on student completion of assignments is rudimentary and only partially effective.	Teacher's system for maintaining information on student completion of assignments is fully effective.	Teacher's system for maintaining information on student completion of assignments is fully effective. Students participate in the maintenance of records.
Student Progress in Learning	Teacher has no system for maintaining information on student progress in learning, or the system is in disarray.	Teacher's system for maintaining information on student progress in learning is rudimentary and partially effective.	Teacher's system for maintaining information on student progress in learning is effective.	Teacher's system for maintaining information on student progress in learning is fully effective. Students contribute information and interpretation of the records.
Non-Instructional Records	Teacher's records for non-instructional activities are in disarray, resulting in errors and confusion.	Teacher's records for non-instructional activities are adequate, but they require frequent monitoring to avoid error.	Teacher's system for maintaining information on non-instructional activities is fully effective.	Teacher's system for maintaining information on non-instructional activities is highly effective, and students contribute to its maintenance.

Figure 9.5.
Summary Rubric for Domain 4

DOMAIN 4: PROFESSIONAL RESPONSIBILITIES
Component 4c: Communicating With Families

Elements: Information about the instructional program • Information about individual students
• Engagement of families in the instructional program

LEVEL OF PERFORMANCE

ELEMENT	UNSATISFACTORY	BASIC	PROFICIENT	DISTINGUISHED
Information About the Instructional Program	Teacher provides little information about the instructional program to families.	Teacher participates in the school's activities for parent communication but offers little additional information.	Teacher provides frequent information to parents, as appropriate, about the instructional program.	Teacher provides frequent information to parents, as appropriate, about the instructional programs. Students participate in preparing materials for their families.
Information About Individual Students	Teacher provides minimal information to parents and does not respond or responds insensitively to parent concerns about students.	Teacher adheres to the school's required procedures for communicating to parents. Responses to parent concerns are minimal.	Teacher communicates with parents about students' progress on a regular basis and is available as needed to respond to parent concerns.	Teacher provides information to parents frequently on both positive and negative aspects of student progress. Responses to parent concerns are handled with great sensitivity.
Engagement of Families in the Instructional Program	Teacher makes no attempt to engage families in the instructional program, or such attempts are inappropriate.	Teacher makes modest and inconsistently successful attempts to engage families in the instructional program.	Teacher's efforts to engage families in the instructional program are frequent and successful.	Teacher's efforts to engage families in the instructional program are frequent and successful. Students contribute ideas for projects that will be enhanced by family participation.

DOMAIN 4: PROFESSIONAL RESPONSIBILITIES
Component 4d: Contributing to the School and District

Elements: Relationships with colleagues • Service to the school • Participation in school and district projects

LEVEL OF PERFORMANCE

ELEMENT	UNSATISFACTORY	BASIC	PROFICIENT	DISTINGUISHED
Relationships With Colleagues	Teacher's relationships with colleagues are negative or self-serving.	Teacher maintains cordial relationships with colleagues to fulfill the duties that the school or district requires.	Support and cooperation characterize relationships with colleagues.	Support and cooperation characterize relationships with colleagues. Teacher takes initiative in assuming leadership among the faculty.
Service to the School	Teacher avoids becoming involved in school events.	Teacher participates in school events when specifically asked.	Teacher volunteers to participate in school events, making a substantial contribution.	Teacher volunteers to participate in school events, making a substantial contribution, and assumes a leadership role in at least some aspect of school life.
Participation in School and District Projects	Teacher avoids becoming involved in school and district projects.	Teacher participates in school and district projects when specifically asked.	Teacher volunteers to participate in school and district projects, making a substantial contribution.	Teacher volunteers to participate in school and district projects, making a substantial contribution, and assumes a leadership role in a major school or district project.

Figure 9.5.
Continued

DOMAIN 4: PROFESSIONAL RESPONSIBILITIES
Component 4e: Growing and Developing Professionally
Elements: Enhancement of content knowledge and pedagogical skill ● Service to the profession

LEVEL OF PERFORMANCE

ELEMENT	UNSATISFACTORY	BASIC	PROFICIENT	DISTINGUISHED
Enhancement of Content Knowledge and Pedagogical Skill	Teacher engages in no professional development activities to enhance knowledge or skill.	Teacher participates in professional activities to a limited extent when they are convenient.	Teacher seeks out opportunities for professional development to enhance content knowledge and pedagogical skill.	Teacher seeks out opportunities for professional development and makes a systematic attempt to conduct action research in his classroom.
Service to the Profession	Teacher makes no effort to share knowledge with others or to assume professional responsibilities.	Teacher finds limited ways to contribute to the profession.	Teacher participates actively in assisting other educators.	Teacher initiates important activities to contribute to the profession, such as mentoring new teachers, writing articles for publication, and making presentations.

DOMAIN 4: PROFESSIONAL RESPONSIBILITIES
Component 4f: Showing Professionalism
Elements: Service to students ● Advocacy ● Decision making

LEVEL OF PERFORMANCE

ELEMENT	UNSATISFACTORY	BASIC	PROFICIENT	DISTINGUISHED
Service to Students	Teacher is not alert to students' needs.	Teacher's attempts to serve students are inconsistent.	Teacher is moderately active in serving students.	Teacher is highly proactive in serving students, seeking out resources when necessary.
Advocacy	Teacher contributes to school practices that result in some students being ill-served by the school.	Teacher does not knowingly contribute to some students being ill-served by the school.	Teacher works within the context of a particular team or department to ensure that all students receive a fair opportunity to succeed.	Teacher makes a particular effort to challenge negative attitudes and helps ensure that all students, particularly those traditionally under-served, are honored in the school.
Decision Making	Teacher makes decisions based on self-serving interests.	Teacher's decisions are based on limited, though genuinely professional, considerations.	Teacher maintains an open mind and participates in team or department decision making.	Teacher takes a leadership role in team or departmental decision making and helps ensure that such decisions are based on the highest professional standards.

Figure 9.5.
Continued

CHAPTER TEN

Structures, Processes, and Instruments for Teacher Reflection and Examination of Practice

I n this chapter, a specific process is described for each of the three teacher types I previously identified:

- Experienced teacher

- Beginning or transferring teacher

- Marginal teacher

Process for the Experienced Teacher

The focus of work with the experienced teacher is on professional growth and continued development of teaching expertise. Self-reflection on practice leads to questions about teaching or identification of problem areas. Reflection is aided by familiarity with Danielson's (1996) Framework for Teaching. Teachers engage in professional growth for 2 years and then evaluation in the 3rd year. In the first 2 months of the school year, I send out (a) a memo (such as the one shown in Figure 10.1), (b) the Professional Growth Worksheet (Figure 10.2), and (c) the direction sheet Experienced Teachers' Professional Growth to my Year 1 and 2 teachers, along with ancillary pages (see Figures 10.4 through 10.7). When beginning this system, I sorted my experienced teachers and put equal numbers into Professional Growth Year 1, Professional Growth Year 2, and Evaluation Year 3. (After this point, teachers follow the natural cycle, but their individual starting points were decided arbitrarily.)

After teachers have completed the Professional Growth Worksheet, they make an appointment to talk with me and share their work. These are exciting and stimulating conversations because I am able to understand what is of interest to them and is motivating them. This

(text continues on page 84)

Memorandum

To: Professional Growth Year Teachers
From: Dan
Date: October 1, 1999
Re: Goal setting for professional growth

Please review the following sections in the *Growth-Focused Evaluation System* (GFES) notebook:

Teacher Professional Growth Years 1 & 2

After reflection, select one of two categories: Big Picture Option or Standards-Based Goals. (You will work in the other area next year.)

Once you have selected a category, choose from the three activities listed under the title. Follow the steps listed under that activity as you work on your goal.

It is also appropriate to follow up on a previous year's goal. Please recall that I am assigning everyone one goal that we have already discussed: Complete the technology staff development checklist and review it with our tech coordinator. I have attached a copy of the checklist to this memo. Please list this goal on the Professional Growth Worksheet too.

Please make an appointment with me soon to review the goals that you have selected. You should come to the conference with the goals articulated on the Professional Growth Worksheet (also attached.) If you have any questions, I would be happy to help you in any way.

Thanks for your attention to this matter.

Figure 10.1.
Sample Administrative Memo for Professional Growth Year Teachers

Professional Growth Worksheet
Growth-Focused Evaluation System

Big Picture Options

○ A. Topic Exploration
○ B. Reflection on General Teaching Practice
○ C. Career and Leadership Development

Standards-Based Goal

○ A. A new goal related to a component in the Framework for Teaching
○ B. A goal identified during Year 3 evaluation process
○ C. Instruction-based project

1. *Choose a category from above: Big Picture Options or Standards-Based Goal.*
2. *Choose A, B, or C under that category.*
3. *Find and complete instructions page for the one you chose.*
4. *List any other goals you will be working on, any assigned building goal, or other goal assigned by your principal.*
5. *At the end of the year, note progress on goals.*
6. *Write down a possible goal for next year.*

Other Goals:

Progress on goals:

Possible goal for next year:

Figure 10.2.
Professional Growth Worksheet

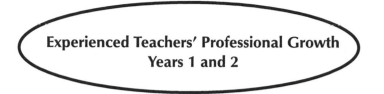

Instructions for teachers to fill out the Professional Growth Worksheet:

1. Choose one of the following categories: Big Picture Option or Standards-Based Goals for Year 1 work and do the other in Year 2.

2. Once you have chosen Big Picture or Standards-Based, make a selection of A, B, or C from within that category. The subpoints are described on the following pages.

3. List the activity on the Professional Growth Worksheet at the end of the Professional Growth Section in the GFES notebook.

<table>
<tr><td>

Big Picture Options

A. Topic Exploration
B. Reflection on General Teaching Practice
C. Career and Leadership Development

</td><td>

Standards-Based Goal

A. A new goal related to a component in the Framework for Teaching
B. A goal identified during Year 3 evaluation process
C. Instruction-based project

</td></tr>
</table>

The three choices under each of the two professional growth categories listed above are further described on the following pages.

Figure 10.3.
Experienced Teachers' Professional Growth, Years 1 and 2

Choice for Year 1 or 2: Big Picture Options

A. TOPIC EXPLORATION

1. Choose a topic from the box below or one of your own choosing.

Topics for Exploration

Brain research   Assessment/portfolios   Differentiated instruction

Inclusion   Multiple intelligence   Constructivism   Arts integration

Tracking/ability grouping   Collaborative learning   Block scheduling

Curriculum integration   Literature circles   Student-centered learning

Project-based learning   School/museum partnerships

---

2. Discuss choice of topic with your principal when you sit down at the beginning of the school year to review plans for the year.
3. Following that meeting, research the topic, exploring at least five sources of information.
4. Write down your reflections on the information and how it could be applied in your teaching situation. Written reflections are to be 1-page minimum in length.
5. Share a copy of reflections with your principal near the end of the school year and place one copy in Section 5 of your GFES notebook.

Figure 10.4.
Choice for Year 1 or 2: Big Picture Options

Choice for Year 1 or 2: Big Picture Options

B. REFLECTION ON GENERAL TEACHING ISSUES

1. Choose a topic from the box below or one of your own choosing.

Considering My Grading and Assessment Practices

Assigning Instructional Priorities

Comparing and Contrasting Methods of Teaching With My Own

Curriculum Development in My Classroom

Appropriate Levels of Parental Involvement

Implementing Multiple Intelligences/Brain Research Theory

Providing Integrated Teaching and Learning Experiences

---

2. Discuss choice of topic with your principal when you sit down at the beginning of the school year to review plans for the year.
3. Following that meeting, research the topic, exploring at least five sources of information.
4. Write down your reflections on the information and how it could be applied in your teaching situation. Written reflections are to be 1-page minimum in length.
5. Share a copy of reflections with your principal near the end of the school year and place one copy in Section 5 of your GFES notebook.

Figure 10.5.
Choice for Year 1 or 2: Big Picture Options

Choice for Year 1 or 2: Big Picture Options

C. CAREER AND LEADERSHIP DEVELOPMENT

1. Goals may be coordinated with an advanced degree program so that there is mutual benefit to improved instruction and the achievement of personal professional goals. For example, work on a thesis related to hands-on science lessons may be implemented in the teacher's classroom and shared with other teachers at the grade level. Share evidence of this work with your principal and include it in Section 5 of your GFES notebook.

2. Significant work in providing curriculum leadership may be an appropriate area of written reflection. Write a paragraph reflecting what you have learned about leadership and best ways to lead others. Share with your principal and include in Section 5 of your GFES notebook.

3. Other examples in this category are, but not limited to, serving as a mentor or peer coach; leading an academic building committee, study group, or a significant level of involvement in the evaluation and/or growth process of another professional. Provide a summary paragraph reflecting on this experience and, after sharing with your principal, place this summary in Section 5 in your GFES notebook.

Figure 10.6.
Choice for Year 1 or 2: Big Picture Options

Choice for Year 1 or 2: Standards-Based Goal

1. Choose one of the following:
   A. Select a new goal for your professional growth related to Domains 1, 2, or 4 of the Framework for Teaching.
   B. Work on a goal that you identified during your Year 3 evaluation process.
   C. Work on a project that relates to an improvement in your instruction of students. For example, redesigning student learning centers, improving a unit of instruction, designing options and methods to differentiate instruction, or working on integration of curriculum.
2. Reflect on the process and note the progress you made during the year on the Professional Growth Worksheet.
3. Share a copy with your principal and place a copy in Section 5 of your GFES notebook.

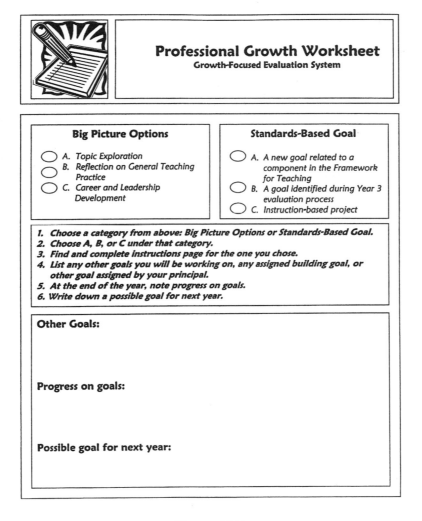

Figure 10.7.
Choice for Year 1 or 2: Standards-Based Goal

allows me to offer suggestions and be on the lookout for ways to assist them in whatever they are working on, such as books, instructional materials, workshops, or community resources. At this time, I also add a goal for them to work on as needed or assign a building or district goal that I expect everyone to work on. If I have gotten feedback from parents about a lack of communication, for example, I will add a specific goal about communication for that teacher to work on during the year.

At the end of the year, I ask the teachers to share with me briefly in written form what progress they have made on the goals they have set. Depending on the teacher and the goals, I may also request that we set a time to discuss the progress in person. This process provides accountability for the teacher and a sense of completion of the process for both of us. We refer back to the goals at the beginning of the next year. Talking with each of the teachers, whether they are engaged in the professional growth or evaluation years, is time very well spent.

Teacher Records of Professional Growth in the Growth-Focused Evaluation System Notebook

As I mentioned above, under the process steps for each professional growth option, teachers must keep a record of the completed work on goals and evaluation analyses in Section 5 of their GFES notebook. If we desire a learning journey for our teachers, we need to have them compile in one place significant markers along the way. The GFE system asks teachers to give thought to this each year. Teacher learning must show connectedness and should not be a haphazard series of unrelated occurrences. Each year, it is easy for the teacher and the principal to refer to the previous year's work and to build upon it. Teachers are able to gain a sense of satisfaction regarding the progress of their own growth and learning in the process. If the district you are a part of has a professional advancement system of some type (e.g., points or credit for workshops or college classes) in place, it makes sense for it to be included as well in Section 5.

Process for the Experienced Teacher: Year 3 Evaluation

In the evaluation during Year 3, I begin the process in the first 2 months of school with my teachers. I send out a memo (Figure 10.8),

Memorandum

To: Evaluation Year Teachers
From: Dan
Date: October 1, 1999
Re: Evaluation process

During the evaluation year, the focus is on teaching practice as summarized in the Professional Teaching Practice Domains area. Please familiarize yourself with this section of the GFES notebook. Use the Evaluation Planning Worksheet (attached) to guide you as you select an area of focus in examining your practice.

First, select a domain from the four. Second, select two components from this domain. Next, formulate two or three questions about your practice as it relates to these components (see the sheet Sample Evaluation Year 3 Questions About Teaching Practice; Domains and Components; Possible Data Collection Instrument). For example, if you had selected Component 3d, Providing Feedback to Students, your question might be "Is my feedback timely, accurate, constructive, and specific?" To obtain data for answering your question, look at the Experienced Teachers' Sample Evaluation Instruments, Year 3 chart to select an instrument. Two instruments (there may be others) that could help you answer the question would be (a) have an observer in your classroom or (b) videotape yourself. You would list this on the last line of the Evaluation Planning Worksheet under "Instrument(s) used."

After you have completed the worksheet or if you have further questions, please set a time to review it with me at your earliest convenience.

Figure 10.8.
Sample Administrative Memo for Evaluation Year Teachers

a worksheet (Figure 10.9), and an example page such as the one in Figure 10.10.

Teachers are asked to formulate questions related to their instruction, such as "Do the assessment techniques I use reflect my beliefs about student learning? Are my questioning and discussion techniques effective? Do I communicate clearly with parents?" Teachers must link their "teaching questions" with components in the Instruction domain found in the Framework for Teaching. After completing the Evaluation Planning Worksheet, a worksheet that states their questions and relates them to the specific component in the framework, teachers set up an appointment with me to discuss the question or questions. Sometimes teachers have an idea of what they want to accomplish but need help formulating the exact question or deciding what component it relates to best. We then discuss what instrument or instruments might be most helpful to get feedback to answer the question. We mutually select an instrument to gain feedback related to the teaching question. Figure 10.11 shows sample instruments for the experienced teacher to use, and the samples are also found in Resource A. They are intended as examples of various types of instruments but could also be used in their current form. I have found it to be a more powerful experience for a teacher to design her or his own instrument to best meet her or his own unique needs.

The initial meeting between teacher and administrator is an opportunity for discussion and problem solving. The teacher subsequently is responsible to go out and complete the work. After the feedback or data have been collected, the teacher must write an analysis of the data, articulate answers to the questions raised, and then write an action plan with appropriate goals for the next year. Following is an example of an analysis that one of my teachers wrote about her experience. She chose an external observer collegial observation type of instrument or method to gain knowledge and information to answer the questions she was raising.

Self-Evaluation Through Peer Observation

It has been my goal this year to develop an approach or method to teach phonics that is effective for student learning and one I am comfortable teaching. Although I firmly believe that children need to know there is a relationship between letter patterns and sound patterns in English, I know I would not be comfortable with an intensive, traditional, skills approach to teaching these patterns.

My preference is to teach phonics strategically, in the meaningful context of reading and enjoying literature and in the

(text continues on page 90)

Evaluation Planning Worksheet
Growth-Focused Evaluation System

Teacher Name _____   Date _____

Selected Domain: _____
(From Professional Teaching Practice Domains)

First component: _____

Second component: _____

Questions about my teaching practice:

1. _____

2. _____

3. _____

Instrument(s) used _____

Figure 10.9.
Evaluation Planning Worksheet

**Sample Evaluation Year 3 Questions About Teaching Practice;
Domains and Components; Possible Data Collection Instruments**

Sample Questions About Teaching Practice	Domain and Components	Possible Data Collection Instruments
1. Are my questioning and discussion techniques effective?	3—Instruction b. Using Questioning/Discussion	Media Recording, External Observer, Student Feedback
2. Do I group my students in ways that enhance instruction?	2—Classroom Environment c. Classroom Procedures	Media Recording, External Observer, Student Feedback
3. Do I manage transitions between lessons effectively?	3—Instruction c. Engaging Students	Media Recording, External Observer, Student Feedback
4. Do parents of my students feel sufficiently involved in their children's education?	4—Professional Responsibility c. Communicating With Families	Parent Feedback
5. Am I integrating the concept of multiple intelligences to the degree I'd like?	1—Planning and Preparation b. Demonstrating Knowledge of Students	Improvement Portfolio
6. Do my teaching methods target different ways of learning?	1—Planning and Preparation b. Demonstrating Knowledge of Students	Student Feedback, Improvement Portfolio
7. Do the assessment techniques I use reflect my beliefs about student learning?	3—Instruction d. Providing Feedback to Students	Improvement Portfolio, Student Feedback, Parent Feedback
8. Is the atmosphere in my classroom one that fosters respect and an easy rapport between the students as well as the students and myself?	2—Classroom Environment a. Respect and Rapport	Media Recording, Student Feedback
9. Have I made the best and safest use of my classroom and its contents, considering the changing needs of my students from one lesson to the next?	2—Classroom Environment e. Organizing Space	External Observer
10. How can I challenge all students? What resources are available? How are others coping with a wide range of academic needs?	1—Planning and Preparation c. Selecting Instructional Goals d. Demonstrating Knowledge of Resources	Improvement Portfolio, Student Performance Data, External Observer, Instruction-Based Project
11. How can I strengthen my reading instruction in the area of phonics from a strategic contextual perspective?	3—Instruction c. Engaging Students in Learning	External Observer, Instruction-Based Project
12. Do I communicate clearly with parents and students?	4—Professional Responsibility c. Communicating With Families	Parent Feedback, External Observer

Figure 10.10.
Sample Evaluation Year 3 Questions About Teaching Practice

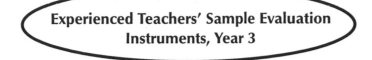

Type of Instrument	Title
External Observer	EO 1
	EO 2
	EO 3
	EO 4
Media Recording	MR 1
	MR 2
Student Feedback	SF 1
	SF 2
	SF 3
Parent Feedback	PF 1
	PF 2
Principal Observation (clinical supervision)	PO 1-A
	PO 1-B
	PO 1-C
Improvement Portfolio	IP
Instruction-Based Project	IBP

Figure 10.11.
Experienced Teachers' Sample Evaluation Instruments, Year 3

context of writing, rather than through intensive, daily skills lessons.

I have been very pleased with Patricia Cunningham's suggested activities and word lists in *Phonics They Use.* I have been pleased with her suggested "word family" lists and been able to connect them to quality literature. For example, the -*ack* sound (e.g., sack, pack) was abundant in the story "Old Black Fly." It was a delightful story—great for chanting musically along with movement and drama. After a writing response activity to "Old Black Fly" (or a science lesson connecting with our study of insects), it was appropriate to revisit the -*ack* sound or chunk of word. The children were ready then to make their own lists of words (*back, lack, crack, stack, black*) and write serious or silly sentences with words from their lists.

These exercises, inspired by Cunningham's book, were so successful (and fun!) that they reinforced my belief that it is easier to learn phonics through whole-to-part teaching (reading and writing first, and seeing words in familiar texts) than it is to learn from part-to-whole (phonics first) teaching.

Because I prefer to teach phonics strategically, I also found the mechanics of spelling and editing best taught in the context of written language. The traditional D.O.L. approach for teaching editing and basic skills never seemed to "carry over" into the students' real writing. When I substituted a written letter on chart paper from teacher to class, however, I found a much stronger transferring of skills and spelling consistency. A meaningful letter (Dear second graders) filled with daily news and events was not only interesting to them but also involved them in a meaningful way with many more of the mechanics and skills of reading and writing successfully.

Despite my satisfaction with these two activities (quality literature to discover word families and class letters for word recognition, spelling, and editing), I still worried about those children weak in decoding skills. I wanted a method of taking an individual word and "chunking" it so that children would learn to look at and, through the whole word, to decode it.

Although it seemed too "part-to-whole" for me, I knew the Glass Analysis program had been highly recommended. I decided to observe a well-respected colleague as she used Glass Analysis with her first graders.

_____'s fast-moving, fun, whole-class involvement sold me on the Glass Analysis method. Not only did _____ move efficiently through a stack of word cards using the Glass procedure as it was intended to be used, but she then took it one step farther.

_____ got the children physically involved by distributing letter cards to many individual children. She had them build words in front of the class with suggestions from those seated. It was fast, fun, and had the attention and involvement of all the children all the time.

For me, seeing _____'s technique of stretching Glass to incorporate a Cunningham approach was the missing link I needed. I know that teaching reading both in context of reading/writing activities and in isolation (as in Glass Analysis) is necessary and effective and provides a balanced literacy instruction.

Observing a colleague in action showed me (in a nonthreatening way) what I was missing. The experience empowered me because I did not just read about it, but I saw and experienced it.

I believe that the observation also benefited _____ by helping her strengthen and refine her method. The dialogue we had about the method's effectiveness will serve to broaden our individual teaching styles and build respect for each other as professionals.

Although it is extremely gratifying to help children learn and grow, it is also exciting to experience the learning I get to do. I have learned a lot in this year and look forward to all I will learn in the next years.

May, 1997

SOURCE: This unpublished self-evaluation analysis is printed with permission from its author, Ruth Evenhouse.

When the teacher analysis is ready, teacher and principal sit down and discuss the results together. This is another great opportunity for discussion of professional practice. I have found these times to be very invigorating as teachers discuss how they have reflected on their practice, interpreted related data, and then made further plans. I have found that we have gotten into much more substantive issues than I ever did using traditional techniques.

Prior to this meeting I have also prepared general comments related to the teacher's professional practice. I tell the teachers it is part of my responsibility as supervisor to give comments, but I limit my remarks to areas about which I feel qualified to comment—professional responsibilities like curriculum work, school leadership, peer interactions, parent feedback I've received, and collegiality. As needed, I also include a goal for them to work on. If teachers have inaccurate self-perceptions or miss larger issues that need to be dealt with, this conference is a time to bring those issues to the forefront in a thoughtful and tactful way.

Most of all, this meeting is a time to celebrate the positive performance of teachers and to build on their strengths. Through celebrating strengths, administrators can build up teachers in genuine ways, as well as increase their capacity to change and envision future success. We are all encouraged to development further by words of encouragement that build on our strengths. Our words do matter; we must choose them carefully for the maximum impact as we seek to communicate suggestions or give well-earned praise to our teachers. An example of a principal analysis follows:

Sample Principal Summary for Jill Brown

April 21, 20___

Jill, you have done a great job with your self-evaluation this year. I think you should be very pleased with the results of your parent survey. You did a typically excellent and thorough job of putting together the survey and compiling the data. Your observations and reflections were right on target. What really came through as I looked over the results is that you love and care for the children in your classroom while at the same time maintaining a positive and well-disciplined classroom atmosphere. Outstanding!

I have really appreciated your calm, even-tempered attitude that you have shown in working with other staff members. You consistently display a "can-do" attitude and think and expect the best from others, although not naively so. You always seem ready to jump in and do your share or more.

I encourage you to continue to grow in the areas of technology and mathematics so that you can share with others at your grade level as well. I have appreciated the leadership you have provided and your flexibility in different situations. You are open to trying new things and lead others by your example.

You have expanded yourself professionally so that you work comfortably and competently with students on either end of the ability spectrum. Your work this year with Rob and his parents in meeting his needs has inspired confidence in them about our school and our district.

Thank you for your work on the Language Arts and Reading Incentive Committees this past year. Your opinions, based on your experience at two different grade levels, have been very helpful. I know that I can always count on you to state your opinions with tact, good judgment, and honesty. You consistently are able to look at things from the students' perspective so that the experiences planned are meaningful for them.

Jill, you have much to offer both inside and outside the classroom, and I encourage you to pick and choose your involvement carefully so that you avoid burnout. Your leadership and people skills, good ideas, sensitivity, and willingness to work things out make you a valuable professional in our school community. I also encourage you to continue to develop these skills and am ready to assist you in whatever ways possible. May you continue to find meaning, growth, and joy in your work as you serve students and parents.

Sincerely,

◄◦►

A summary of the 3-year process for the experienced teacher is shown in Figure 10.12.

Administrators' Summary Plan for Implementing the Growth-Focused Evaluation System With Experienced Teachers

Timeline for Implementation of Steps Listed Below:

September—Steps 1, 2, 3

October—Step 4

March-April—Step 5

Step 1. Consider your teaching staff and three descriptions: (a) beginning (2 or fewer years of experience), (b) experienced (3 or more years of experience), and (c) marginal (to be defined). Determine what category is applicable to each teacher.

Step 2. Divide your experienced teachers into three basically even groups (most teachers will be in this category). Assign them to one of the following groups: (a) Year 1 Professional Growth, (b) Year 2 Professional Growth, and (c) Year 3 Evaluation so that they will not all be on the same step at the same time.

Step 3. If your staff is large enough to merit an assistant principal, then divide and assign evaluation responsibilities. Each of you should have a reasonable amount of people to work with in each of the three

Professional Growth and Evaluation Process
for the Experienced Teacher

Year 1—Professional Growth

1. Become familiar with the two categories: Big Picture Options and Standards-Based Goals.
2. Select one of the categories. Under the category selected, choose one of the activities described. List the category and activity and goals by using the Professional Growth Worksheet.
3. Before the end of October, set an appointment with your principal for a conference to discuss goals chosen. Your principal may suggest additional goals at this time.
4. In the last month of the year, complete the Professional Growth Worksheet to reflect your progress toward, or achievement of, your goals for the year. Select a possible goal for the next year. Submit a copy of the Professional Growth Worksheet to your principal and place your copy in your GFES notebook.

Year 2—Professional Growth

Repeat the above process, except work in the alternate category that you did not choose last year.

Year 3—Evaluation

1. Become familiar with the four Professional Teaching Practice Domains. Select a domain as a general focus area. Within that domain, select at least two components as your focus for evaluation. Construct two or three questions about your teaching practice that you would like answered as you think about those components.
2. Before the end of October, set an appointment with your principal to discuss your focus and questions about teaching practice. Mutually select an appropriate data collection method to help obtain answers to your questions. See Experienced Teachers' Sample Evaluation Instrument, Year 3.
3. Collect data.
4. Do the following: (a) Prepare a written analysis of the data collected, (b) use the data to articulate answers to the teaching practice questions you initially raised, and (c) include a summary discussing your future plans and goals for the following year.
5. Meet with your principal to discuss your results. Your principal will also be prepared at this meeting to share general comments related to your professional practice and performance. Mutually discuss possible goals for professional growth for next year.

Year 4—Professional Growth

Repeat Year 1 above and continue through the cycle.

Figure 10.12.
Professional Growth and Evaluation Process for the Experienced Teacher

categories because you will be working with the whole staff each year. Remember that growth and development of your staff is directly tied to student achievement and is one of the most important things you can do each year to affect student learning.

Step 4: Professional Growth Years 1 and 2. Send out a memo (see Figure 10.1 for example) and the Professional Growth Worksheet (Figure 10.2). Teachers will select a category and then an activity under that category. They should write these choices down on the Professional Growth Worksheet and then make an appointment to see you for a brief meeting. This meeting is your opportunity to assign them an additional goal as you see fit or to redirect them if needed. Determine in your own mind what category and activity may be most appropriate for them to work in. For you to be most effective as a principal, *you must know what your teacher needs most and also have a command of the domains and evaluation instruments so that you can give meaningful guidance.*

Step 4: Evaluation Year 3. This section is similar to the process above except that the focus needs to be on the domains from the Framework for Teaching (found in Chapter 9). When you send out the memo to remind teachers to start the process (beginning of the year), include the Evaluation Planning Worksheet (Figure 10.9). After the teachers have reflected on the domains, they should be able to come to you having selected one of the four domains to work in and within that domain two components for their focus. It is important that they prepare two or three questions; we are attempting to get them to reflect and self-assess. Don't shortchange this step! After you have talked with them (again, this is an opportunity to add a question or two based on what you believe a needed growth area may be for them), then discuss together what instrument would work best to achieve satisfactory answers to the questions. The teachers then collect data and follow the suggested sequence: written analysis of the data, answers to questions, summary including future plans and goals.

Step 5: Professional Growth Years 1 and 2. Review completed copies of the Professional Growth Worksheets. Each of the teachers should give you a copy and put a copy in Section 5 of their GFES notebooks. Make sure they have selected a goal for next year. Meet with them only if you desire to comment or clarify.

Step 5: Evaluation Year 3. Meet with teachers to review their self-evaluations, which should include the following: (a) original questions, (b) instrument used for data collection, (c) analysis of data, and (d) discussion of future plans and goals. It is important that you come to this meeting prepared to share in written (preferable) or oral form any comments relating to the teachers' professional practice and performance. These will be general in nature—for example, your perceptions of their strengths and weaknesses; feedback you receive from parents, students, and other colleagues; how they function as team members; how they carry out professional responsibilities. Because these are your experienced teachers, this meeting is a great opportunity for encouragement and positive reinforcement. You should keep copies of all work, and the teachers should also keep copies in Section 5 of their GFES notebooks.

General Comments. It is important to be connected to the growth of each person every year to assist in individual and group development. You will spend more time in conversation with each teacher than under older systems. Some of this time will be available, though, because you are spending less time sitting and evaluating in the classroom. This is not to say that you need not appear in classrooms; it is advisable to get into classrooms whenever possible for brief periods, but more effort should be expended on meaningful conversations that involve self-reflection on the teacher's part.

Process for the Beginning and Transferring Teacher

The induction of a new teacher into the profession and the local setting is a process that demands significant support to ensure the success of the teacher and her or his students. During this time, the administrator is seeking to provide further training and support but is also forming a summative opinion about the teacher's capabilities. Although the goal is to make the teacher successful, the administrator must also be prepared to address any serious deficiencies and to move to nonrenewal of contract if needed. To achieve these goals, classroom observations will be made according to the following schedule:

- *Year 1.* Minimum of two formal written observations during the first semester and one in the second semester. Administrators should make several informal visits during the first 2 months of school to ensure that everything is going smoothly.

- *Year 2.* Minimum of two formal written observations during the first semester and one in the second semester.

- *Year 3.* If satisfactory evaluations have been recorded in the first 2 years, the teacher may be moved into the experienced teacher 3-year cycle. Administrators need to be in close contact with those experienced teachers who are new to the system for many of the same reasons stated for the beginning teacher. Adjustments to new environments, students, colleagues, and expectations are similar, but it is expected that, with past experience to draw on, the experienced transfer will need less long-term support. It is essential for the administrator to be confident of, and familiar with, the teaching practices of new transfers and to be able to come to summative conclusions about their long-term effectiveness.

- *Years 1 and 2.* Minimum of two formal observations by the administrator using the clinical supervision process.

- *Year 3.* If satisfactory evaluations have been recorded in the first 2 years, the teacher may be moved into the experienced teacher 3-year cycle.

With both beginning and transferring teachers, the clinical supervision model works well to help the principal and teacher begin initial conversations about instruction and classroom climate. Sample pages for this process are shown in Figures 10.13 through 10.16 and are also found in Resource A.

Helpful examples for classroom observation are also found in the Framework for Teaching. During the first 2 years, it is recommended that, through further training, the beginning teacher become very familiar with the Framework for Teaching.

Other helpful resources for administrators and beginning teachers are *The Skillful Teacher: Building Your Teaching Skills* (Saphier & Gower, 1997), *The First Days of School* (Wong, 1998), and ASCD's "How To" Video Series.

Process for the Marginal Teacher

Working with the marginal teacher is not the first choice of any administrator. These situations can best be described by the Japanese symbol for the word *crisis*, which can mean danger or opportunity. Working with teachers on a difficult issue can hold out the opportunity of improvement and growth or, on the danger side, the stiffening of resolve, retribution, and a negative downward spiral that exhausts both principal and teacher.

For starters, bad habits, like weeds, are most easily eliminated when they are small. The goal of the administrator should be to have a positive, healthy, trusting relationship with each staff member so that, when they arise, problems can be dealt with immediately instead of having them grow into large problems or ingrained habits. This calls for an assertive, proactive administrative stance and being in touch with what's really happening in one's school. As I noted in

(text continues on page 102)

Years 1, 2 Evaluation Instruments

PRINCIPAL OBSERVATION
(PO 1-A)

Audience: Intended for use with teachers of Grades K-12; intended for use by administrators.

Action steps: Follow clinical supervision cycle; follow steps listed below.

Analysis needed: Write an analysis of the data you collected. Analysis should include a discussion of possible future changes in teaching practice.

Principal Observation Steps Using the Clinical Supervision Model

1. Teacher should complete Form PO 1-B (Principal Observation, Preobservation Questions) and Form PO 1-C (Principal Observation, Instructional Focus), which immediately follow this page.
2. Teacher should schedule a meeting with principal to discuss the above two forms. Principal and teacher should agree on the focus of the observation, the instrument to be used, and the time of the observation.
3. Observation takes place.
4. A postconference is held within 48 hours regarding the results of the observation. Principal will give a copy of the notes taken during the observation to the teacher immediately following the observation for the teacher's reflection before the postconference.

Figure 10.13.
Years 1, 2 Evaluation Instruments: Principal Observation (PO 1-A)

PRINCIPAL OBSERVATION
(PO 1-B)
(Preobservation Questions)

Teacher _____ **Class**_____ **Date**_____

1. Where are you in the course (e.g., unit, lesson, page numbers)?

2. What teaching/learning activities will be observed?

3. What skills, attitudes, understandings will be taught? (What are your students going to get out of it?)

4. How are you going to do it? What methods you will use?

5. What, if any, particular teaching behaviors do you especially want monitored?

6. How are you going to know whether the students have learned?

7. What special characteristics/needs of the students should be noted?

8. Anything else we need to discuss?

Figure 10.14.
Years 1, 2 Evaluation Instruments, Principal Observation
(PO 1-B) (Preobservation Questions)

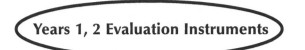

PRINCIPAL OBSERVATION
(PO 1-C)
(Instructional Focus)

Teacher _____ **Class**_____ **Date**_____

Given the focus of the instruction in the lesson and the goals of this observation, what type of observation instrument would best help collect the needed data?

1. *Selective verbatim:* Written record of selected verbal events

2. *Teacher questions:* Written record of questions asked by teacher

3. *Teacher feedback:* Written record of teacher feedback statements to students

4. *Teacher directions and structuring statements:* Written record of the amount, variety, and specificity of directions and structuring statements

5. *Anecdotal records:* Objective notes of classroom interaction and events, looking at the "big picture"

Figure 10.15.
Years 1, 2 Evaluation Instruments, Principal Observation
(PO 1-C) (Instructional Focus)

Professional Growth and Evaluation Process
for the Beginning Teacher

Beginning teachers are defined as follows:

Beginning—no prior teaching experience

Transfer to system—an experienced teacher who has transferred to the system

Expectations for evaluation of the beginning teacher

Classroom observations will be made according to the following schedule:

Year 1. Minimum of two formal written observations during the first semester and one in the second semester. Administrators may make several informal visits during the first 2 months of school to ensure that everything is going smoothly.

Year 2. Minimum of two formal written observations during the first semester and one in the second semester.

Year 3. If satisfactory evaluations have been recorded in the first 2 years, the teacher may be moved into the experienced teacher 3-year cycle.

Expectations for evaluation of the transferring experienced teacher

Years 1 and 2. Minimum of two formal observations by the administrator using the clinical supervision process.

Year 3. If satisfactory evaluations have been recorded in the first 2 years, the teacher may be moved into the experienced teacher 3-year cycle.

Nonrenewal of contract

Nonrenewal decisions may be based on evaluations, enrollment, or budgetary constraints. If evaluations indicate unsatisfactory performance, then the teacher should be assisted according to the RISC plan or terminated. Notification of termination will be given by February 1, and an appeal to the superintendent may be made by March 1.

Figure 10.16.
Professional Growth and Evaluation Process for the Beginning Teacher

Chapter 1, we cannot afford the price of incompetent teaching. To deal effectively with people problems takes resolve and courage. The stronger the relationships with others and the higher the emotional intelligence of the leader, the more effective she or he can be in helping others work on areas of needed improvement.

In my current school system, we recognized that certain teachers required additional encouragement to get serious about needed growth areas, yet the individuals' problems did not merit placement on probation. I am convinced this is the "at-risk" zone where principals too often get bogged down in seeking to improve instruction. There is no clear method of how to proceed, and so principals inwardly throw up their hands in despair. How can we move people along the growth process in a humane and fair way that gives strong assistance, support, and accountability? As I noted in Chapter 8, the *required improvement status category* (RISC) is a proposed idea for improving teacher performance that could happen as well in districts with union contracts. Certainly, in the light of recent (March 1999) California legislation regarding peer review for teachers who have received unsatisfactory evaluations, this is not a radical proposal in any sense. I am personally encouraged by the increasing focus on student needs as opposed to teacher rights, but in some places we still have a long way to go to truly improve and professionalize the teaching profession.

As the superintendent, the director of instruction, and I pondered this question in our school system, we developed the *RISC* plan to help deal with this need. If a teacher is placed in this category, she or he is subject to reduction issues before the successful first-year teacher. This is a category that says, "Let's get serious about these issues," and if insufficient progress is made, probation is the next step. Possible scenarios are represented graphically in Figure 10.17 and are described in writing in Figure 10.18.

Plans for dealing with the marginal teacher will vary by district and contract. What has been developed and explained here is simply one example of a model that works well and is fair in a given situation.

Within our system, we have also developed a process for the probationary teacher. This is included in Figure 10.19 as an example and to complete the entire GFE system. An excellent book that I recommend for practitioners is *The Marginal Teacher: A Step-by-Step Guide to Fair Procedures for Identification and Dismissal* (Lawrence, Vachon, Leake, & Leake, 1993). It is a step-by-step guide through the probationary process for administrators.

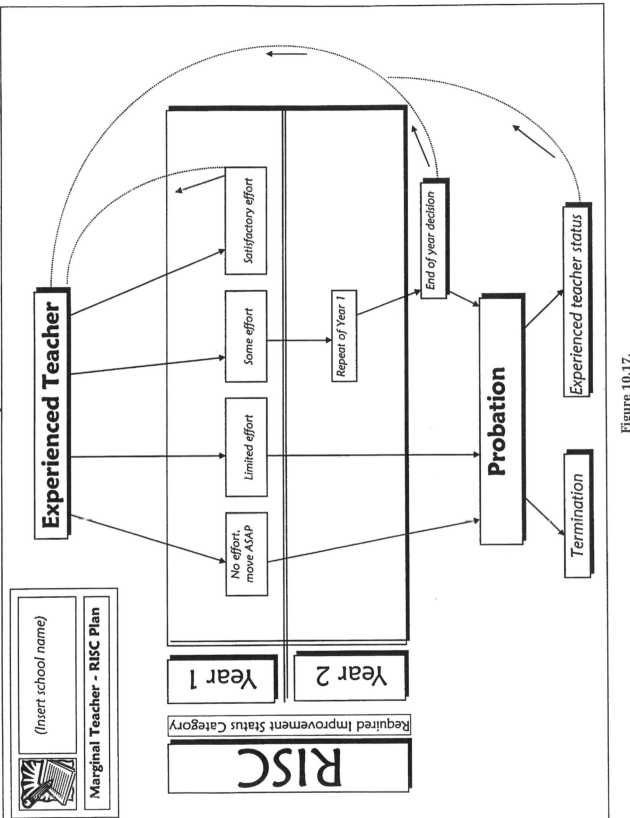

Figure 10.17.
Marginal Teacher—RISC Plan

103

Professional Growth and Evaluation Process
for the Marginal Teacher

1. When an experienced teacher is demonstrating insufficient growth or serious deficiencies in her or his professional practice, she or he will be placed in RISC (required improvement status category). RISC is designed to be a period of intensive assistance for the experienced teacher. Significant effort must be demonstrated by the teacher to show improvement. Administration also provides significant assistance and support to the teacher to aid in the improvement process.

2. RISC is a maximum 2-year process. Teacher placement decisions will be made by administration in communication with the Education Committee.

3. When placed in RISC, four categories are possible, and placement into a category is dependent on teacher response and growth as determined by administration:

   a. Teacher shows no effort and does not respond to, or resists remediation—moved immediately into the probation process, or in extreme cases terminated as soon as possible. Typically, this decision must be made in September or October so that appropriate measures can be taken and due process can be followed.

   b. Teacher shows limited effort toward remediation of problem areas. After Year 1, the decision would be to give the teacher a probationary year contract.

   c. Teacher shows some effort toward remediation of problem areas. The decision at the end of the year would be to have the teacher continue in a second year of RISC, receiving intensive remediation. At the end of Year 2, a decision would be made whether the teacher has made significant enough improvement to return to the experienced teacher category or whether she or he would enter probation year status.

   d. Teacher shows satisfactory improvement in identified problem areas and after 1 year can be returned to the experienced teacher category.

4. Teachers placed on probation will follow the process laid out on the following pages. *Probation* is a period of intensive assistance and due process in a last attempt to assist the teacher to reach a satisfactory level of performance. This period is not to exceed 1 year; typically, the teacher who begins the year in probation may receive notice of intention of termination by January if progress is not demonstrated. Teachers who demonstrate significant and satisfactory improvement may be returned to the experienced teacher category.

Figure 10.18.
Professional Growth and Evaluation Process for the Marginal Teacher

Professional Growth and Evaluation Process
for the Probationary Teacher

1. The process of probation is a period of intensive assistance and due process in a final attempt to assist the teacher to reach a satisfactory level of performance and/or conduct. This period is not to exceed 1 year; typically, the teacher who begins the year in probation will receive notice of intention of termination by January if sufficient progress is not demonstrated. Teachers who demonstrate significant and satisfactory improvement may be returned to the experienced teacher category. The process for teachers and administrators to follow in a probationary year is listed below.

2. The teacher will be notified of probationary status. The building administrator will review recommendations for improvement with the teacher at the appropriate time and provide assistance plans. Most often, this will occur at the beginning of the year when a teacher has been in the RISC category the year before. In more severe cases, however, the process may be accelerated and take place at any time in the year. An accelerated process will follow similar steps as listed below except on an accelerated time frame.

3. A probationary teacher's intensive assistance plans may include (a) observation of another teacher for a day in the same school and another school for a day, (b) assistance by another teacher for a day in the probationary teacher's classroom, (c) attendance at appropriate workshops, (d) helpful articles and videos, and (e) recommendations from administrator observations.

4. Administrators will conduct a minimum of two classroom observations per month during the months of September through December, using the clinical supervision model. These observations will include identified areas of weakness and recommendations for improvement and state a reasonable amount of time for improvement. Administrators involved in the observations will include the building principal and other qualified designees. Part of the observation process may include collecting from the teacher samples of assignments given to students and discipline referral records.

5. If a teacher's performance does not improve, he or she will receive a letter in December, stating the possibility of an unsatisfactory final evaluation with recommendation for dismissal if his or her performance does not improve by January 15.

6. An unsatisfactory final evaluation meeting will be conducted in January with the teacher and the Education Committee of the school board. If the Education Committee approves the termination of the contract, this will take the form of a recommendation to the school board.

7. The school board will act on the recommendation, and its decision will be considered final.

Figure 10.19.
Professional Growth and Evaluation Process for the Probationary Teacher

Guidelines for Termination of Contract

1. Grounds for termination must be put in writing by the principal and other evaluators and be presented to the staff member, Education Committee, superintendent, and school board.

2. The staff member will be granted a hearing before each authority dealing with the matter (Education Committee and school board) and will be given adequate notice of times of all meetings.

3. Both the staff member and the authority dealing with the matter may have a counselor present.

4. Each authority dealing with the matter must act promptly and present its decision in writing to the staff member involved.

SOURCE: A primary reference for the process above and the sample documents was *The Marginal Teacher: A Step-by-Step Guide to Fair Procedures for Identification and Dismissal*, by C. E. Lawrence, M. K. Vachon, D. O. Leake, and B. H. Leake, 1993, Newbury Park, CA: Corwin.

Figure 10.19.
Continued

CHAPTER ELEVEN

Reporting Teacher Evaluation and Professional Growth

The Growth-Focused Evaluation System (GFES) increases the amount of time that teachers and principals spend in professional conversations about teaching and learning. It is helpful for the outcomes (the professional goals and evaluation questions chosen by the teachers) of those conversations to be summarized in one place. Such a summary may be helpful for several reasons:

- It allows the principal to see the interests and needs of the faculty for building staff development.

- It can be forwarded to whoever is in charge of staff development at the district level so that, with summaries from other buildings, the person in charge can get a big picture look at the district's staff development needs.

- It can be requested by the superintendent as an accountability measure from the principals to ensure that the professional development and evaluation process is being carried out.

- It can be shared with board of education members, as appropriate, to demonstrate the kinds of learning and growth occurring among the faculty and to show accountability in supervision.

Examples of the following summary sheets are provided in Resource A:

- Professional Growth and Evaluation Faculty Summary cover page

- Years 1 and 2 Professional Growth Teacher Summary form

- Year 3 Evaluation Teacher Summary form

- Beginning Teacher Evaluation Summary form

- Marginal Teacher Evaluation Summary form

CHAPTER TWELVE

Developing Your Own Evaluation and Professional Growth Plan: Action Steps

Even though you can use this system as it comes prepackaged, I believe that benefits can be gained if you use it as a springboard to engage in a process of reflection, discussion, and then action. Examine by yourself or with others your level of dissatisfaction with your current system. Be honest about the level of effectiveness of your current system in helping teachers and students grow. Use the chapter on leadership (Chapter 4) to reflect on whether current leadership theory is something you can buy into. Does the Growth-Focused Evaluation (GFE) system or what you are currently using better reflect your personal leadership philosophy? Consider what kind of system of evaluation and professional growth will work in your environment, what the potential obstacles may be, and what the political ramifications are. Plan purposefully, gain group consensus, and determine to step out into some new directions.

Within this book, I have suggested the most helpful, up-to-date resource materials I am aware of to assist you in the process of designing your own plan if that is your desire. If you want to reproduce and use the GFE system as I have laid it out in the previous chapters, you are free to do so (with the exception of the Framework—I suggest you purchase a copy for each teacher—it is well worth it!) and will find all the forms you need in the Resource A. I have divided the Resource A forms into five sections (as noted in the beginning of Resource A) that can easily be assembled into a three-ring notebook with five tab dividers. They are in the order needed for the notebook.

Although you are most familiar with the steps you need to take before implementing a new system of evaluation with your superintendent or school board, I urge you to get started in some small and safe ways. Start by giving some choices about the evaluation process to your most excellent and trusted teachers. Discuss with them the questions that are going through their minds about how to improve instruction and develop ways to gain data to answer the questions.

Start with invitations rather than mandates. Find a colleague who shares your conviction for change and reflect together about what works. Share successes and failures as you learn together. Model for your teachers the learning process that you expect of them. Be honest with them about how you really feel about the old way of evaluation and how you would like to learn new approaches along with them. After you have experienced some successes using the methods described in this book, I guarantee that you will not want to continue with the old ways! You more than likely will want to share with administrators and teachers the excitement of what you are doing and ultimately change your entire system of evaluation.

Best wishes for an invigorating and productive journey of discovery!

Resource A

Growth-Focused Evaluation System Sample Documents

Sample documents may be reproduced for use in a single building.

To assemble your Growth-Focused Evaluation System (GFES) notebook, copy the following pages, assembling them with labeled tabs in a three-ring binder:

Growth-Focused Evaluation System Title Page

Tab 1: Introduction

Introduction and Purpose

Rationale for Self-Assessment and Evaluation

GFES Professional Growth and Evaluation Overview

Tab 2: Experienced Teacher Process

Professional Growth and Evaluation Process for the Experienced Teacher

Professional Growth Worksheet

Experienced Teachers' Professional Growth Years 1 and 2 Instructions

Big Picture Options

- Option A: Topic Exploration
- Option B: Reflection on General Teaching Issues
- Option C: Career and Leadership Development

Choice for Year 1 or 2: Standards-Based Goal

Evaluation Planning Worksheet

Sample Evaluation Year 3 Teacher Questions About Teaching Practice; Domains and Concepts; Possible Data Collection Instruments

Experienced Teachers' Sample Evaluation Instruments, Year 3

Year 3 Evaluation Instruments
- External Observer #1-4
- Media Recording #1-2
- Student Feedback #1-3
- Parent Feedback #1-2
- Principal Observation #1 A-C
- Improvement Portfolio
- Instruction-Based Project

Tab 3: Beginning and Transferring Teacher Process

Professional Growth and Evaluation Process for the Beginning Teacher

Sample Evaluation Instruments for the Beginning and Transferring Teacher:
- Principal Observation Process (PO 1-A)
- Preobservation Worksheet (PO 1-B)
- Instructional Focus (PO 1-C)

Tab 4: Marginal and Probationary Teacher Process

Marginal Teacher—RISC Plan

Professional Growth and Evaluation Process for the Marginal Teacher

Professional Growth and Evaluation Process for the Probationary Teacher

Tab 5: Teacher Record of Professional Growth

(Initially, no pages follow this tab. Teachers will insert their completed work.)

Forms for Administrative Use:

Professional Growth Year Teachers (principal memo to teachers)

Evaluation Year Teachers (principal memo to teachers)

Probationary Teacher Observation Record

Professional Growth and Evaluation Faculty Summary Report Cover

Years 1 & 2 Professional Growth Teacher Summary

Year 3 Evaluation Teacher Summary

Beginning Teacher Evaluation Summary

Marginal Teacher Evaluation Summary

(Insert name of school here)

Growth-Focused

Evaluation System

Resource Figure A.1.

Introduction and Purpose

Growth-Focused Evaluation System

Teaching is a complex endeavor. Many intellectual, emotional, spiritual, and physical demands are placed on teachers as they seek to choose appropriate resources, teaching methods, and assessment techniques to make learning meaningful for each student. Classroom environment, planning and preparation, and other professional obligations and responsibilities are essential components in student instruction. It is the intent of this system to assist teachers as they consider how to achieve excellence in their instruction and development as professionals. Included in this notebook are growth and evaluation processes, self-evaluation instruments to aid growth, and an ongoing record of professional growth progress.

The purposes of this growth-focused evaluation system (GFES) notebook are several:

- It seeks to articulate a process for sustained professional growth.

- It offers a variety of methods and strategies for growth and accountability.

- It provides a record of professional growth over a period of years and ultimately, we hope, provides a tool for professional conversation so that together, as teachers and administrators, we may communicate about excellence for students.

Resource Figure A.2.

Rationale for Self-Assessment and Evaluation

The reason for self-assessment and evaluation for the experienced teacher is to encourage and sustain professional growth. As professional educators, we are constantly evaluating ourselves as we interact with students, parents, and peers. It is helpful and necessary as well to engage periodically in a more formal process that gives us time to reflect on recognized excellence in teaching, practice, personal professional growth goals, and/or building or district goals.

Although the self-reflection processes and instruments contained in this document are primarily for experienced teachers, beginning teachers and those who need to strive for defined growth can also make good use of the materials found on the following pages.

Resource Figure A.3.

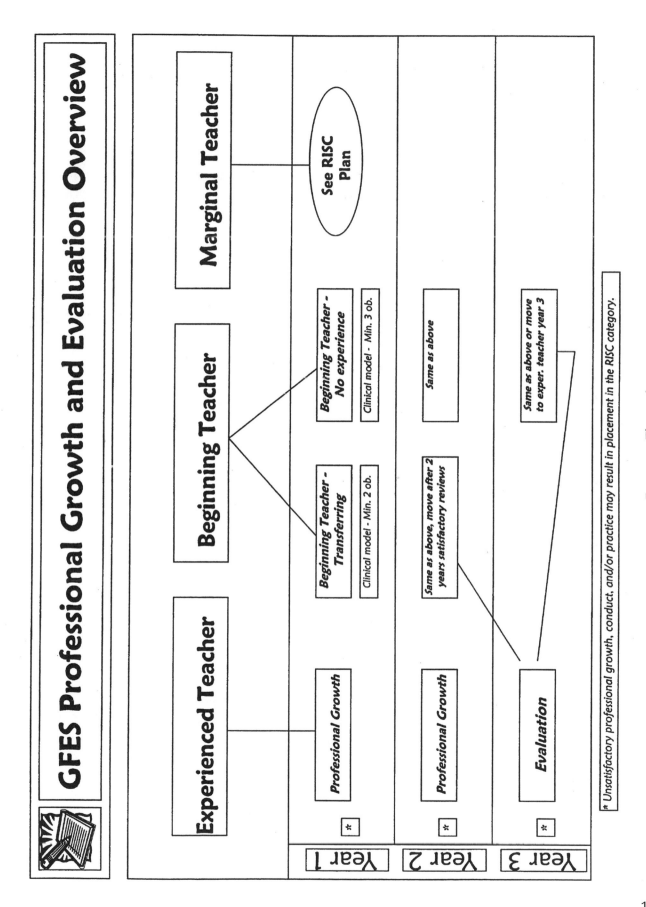

GFES Professional Growth and Evaluation Overview

Experienced Teacher

Beginning Teacher

Marginal Teacher

See RISC Plan

Beginning Teacher - Transferring

Clinical model - Min. 2 ob.

Beginning Teacher - No experience

Clinical model - Min. 3 ob.

Professional Growth

Same as above, move after 2 years satisfactory reviews

Same as above

Professional Growth

Evaluation

Same as above or move to exper. teacher year 3

Year 1 *

Year 2 *

Year 3 *

* *Unsatisfactory professional growth, conduct, and/or practice may result in placement in the RISC category.*

Resource Figure A.4.

115

Professional Growth and Evaluation Process for the Experienced Teacher

Year 1—Professional Growth

1. Become familiar with the two categories: Big Picture Options and Standards-Based Goals.
2. Select one of the categories. Under the category selected, choose one of the activities described. List the category and activity and goals by using the Professional Growth Worksheet.
3. Before the end of October, set an appointment with your principal for a conference to discuss goals chosen. Your principal may suggest additional goals at this time.
4. In the last month of the year, complete the Professional Growth Worksheet to reflect your progress toward, or achievement of, your goals for the year. Select a possible goal for the next year. Submit a copy of the Professional Growth Worksheet to your principal and place your copy in your GFES notebook.

Year 2—Professional Growth

Repeat the above process, except work in the alternate category that you did not choose last year.

Year 3—Evaluation

1. Become familiar with the four Professional Teaching Practice Domains. Select a domain as a general focus area. Within that domain, select at least two components as your focus for evaluation. Construct two or three questions about your teaching practice that you would like answered as you think about those components.
2. Before the end of October, set an appointment with your principal to discuss your focus and questions about teaching practice. Mutually select an appropriate data collection method to help obtain answers to your questions. See Experienced Teachers' Sample Evaluation Instrument, Year 3.
3. Collect data.
4. Do the following: (a) Prepare a written analysis of the data collected, (b) use the data to articulate answers to the teaching practice questions you initially raised, and (c) include a summary discussing your future plans and goals for the following year.
5. Meet with your principal to discuss your results. Your principal will also be prepared at this meeting to share general comments related to your professional practice and performance. Mutually discuss possible goals for professional growth for next year.

Year 4—Professional Growth

Repeat Year 1 above and continue through the cycle.

Resource Figure A.5.
Professional Growth and Evaluation Process for the Experienced Teacher

Professional Growth Worksheet
Growth-Focused Evaluation System

Big Picture Options

○ A. Topic Exploration
○ B. Reflection on General Teaching
        Practice
○ C. Career and Leadership
        Development

Standards-Based Goal

○ A. A new goal related to a
        component in the Framework
        for Teaching
○ B. A goal identified during Year 3
        evaluation process
○ C. Instruction-based project

1. *Choose a category from above: Big Picture Options or Standards-Based Goal.*
2. *Choose A, B, or C under that category.*
3. *Find and complete instructions page for the one you chose.*
4. *List any other goals you will be working on, any assigned building goal, or
    other goal assigned by your principal.*
5. *At the end of the year, note progress on goals.*
6. *Write down a possible goal for next year.*

Other Goals:

Progress on goals:

Possible goal for next year:

Resource Figure A.6.
Professional Growth Worksheet

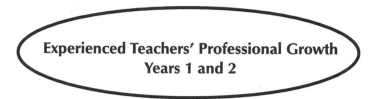

Instructions for teachers to fill out the Professional Growth Worksheet:

1. Choose one of the following categories: Big Picture Option or Standards-Based Goals for Year 1 work and do the other in Year 2.

2. Once you have chosen Big Picture or Standards-Based, make a selection of A, B, or C from within that category. The subpoints are described on the following pages.

3. List the activity on the Professional Growth Worksheet at the end of the Professional Growth Section in the GFES notebook.

Big Picture Options	**Standards-Based Goal**
A. Topic Exploration B. Reflection on General Teaching Practice C. Career and Leadership Development	A. A new goal related to a component in the Framework for Teaching B. A goal identified during Year 3 evaluation process C. Instruction-based project

The three choices under each of the two professional growth categories listed above are further described on the following pages.

Resource Figure A.7.
Experienced Teachers' Professional Growth, Years 1 and 2

Choice for Year 1 or 2: Big Picture Options

A. TOPIC EXPLORATION

1. Choose a topic from the box below or one of your own choosing.

Topics for Exploration

Brain research   Assessment/portfolios   Differentiated instruction

Inclusion   Multiple intelligence   Constructivism   Arts integration

Tracking/ability grouping   Collaborative learning   Block scheduling

Curriculum integration   Literature circles   Student-centered learning

Project-based learning   School/museum partnerships

---

2. Discuss choice of topic with your principal when you sit down at the beginning of the school year to review plans for the year.
3. Following that meeting, research the topic, exploring at least five sources of information.
4. Write down your reflections on the information and how it could be applied in your teaching situation. Written reflections are to be 1-page minimum in length.
5. Share a copy of reflections with your principal near the end of the school year and place one copy in Section 5 of your GFES notebook.

Resource Figure A.8.
Choice for Year 1 or 2: Big Picture Options

Choice for Year 1 or 2: Big Picture Options

B. REFLECTION ON GENERAL TEACHING ISSUES

1. Choose a topic from the box below or one of your own choosing.

Considering My Grading and Assessment Practices

Assigning Instructional Priorities

Comparing and Contrasting Methods of Teaching With My Own

Curriculum Development in My Classroom

Appropriate Levels of Parental Involvement

Implementing Multiple Intelligences Theory

Providing Integrated Teaching and Learning Experiences

---

2. Discuss choice of topic with your principal when you sit down at the beginning of the school year to review plans for the year.
3. Following that meeting, research the topic, exploring at least five sources of information.
4. Write down your reflections on the information and how it could be applied in your teaching situation. Written reflections are to be 1-page minimum in length.
5. Share a copy of reflections with your principal near the end of the school year and place one copy in Section 5 of your GFES notebook.

Resource Figure A.9.
Choice for Year 1 or 2: Big Picture Options

Choice for Year 1 or 2: Big Picture Options

C. CAREER AND LEADERSHIP DEVELOPMENT

1. Goals may be coordinated with an advanced degree program so that there is mutual benefit to improved instruction and the achievement of personal professional goals. For example, work on a thesis related to hands-on science lessons may be implemented in the teacher's classroom and shared with other teachers at the grade level. Share evidence of this work with your principal and include it in Section 5 of your GFES notebook.

2. Significant work in providing curriculum leadership may be an appropriate area of written reflection. Write a paragraph reflecting what you have learned about leadership and best ways to lead others. Share with your principal and include in Section 5 of your GFES notebook.

3. Other examples in this category are, but not limited to, serving as a mentor or peer coach; leading an academic building committee, study group, or a significant level of involvement in the evaluation and/or growth process of another professional. Provide a summary paragraph reflecting on this experience and, after sharing with your principal, place this summary in Section 5 in your GFES notebook.

Resource Figure A.10.
Choice for Year 1 or 2: Big Picture Options

Choice for Year 1 or 2: Standards-Based Goal
---

1. Choose one of the following:
   A. Select a new goal for your professional growth related to Domains 1, 2, or 4 of the Framework for Teaching.
   B. Work on a goal that you identified during your Year 3 evaluation process.
   C. Work on a project that relates to an improvement in your instruction of students. For example, redesigning student learning centers, improving a unit of instruction, designing options and methods to differentiate instruction, or working on integration of curriculum.
2. Reflect on the process and note the progress you made during the year on the Professional Growth Worksheet.
3. Share a copy with your principal and place a copy in Section 5 of your GFES notebook.

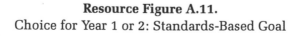

Professional Growth Worksheet
Growth-Focused Evaluation System

Big Picture Options	**Standards-Based Goal**
A. Topic Exploration	A. A new goal related to a component in the Framework for Teaching
B. Reflection on General Teaching Practice	B. A goal identified during Year 3 evaluation process
C. Career and Leadership Development	C. Instruction-based project

1. *Choose a category from above: Big Picture Options or Standards-Based Goal.*
2. *Choose A, B, or C under that category.*
3. *Find and complete instructions page for the one you chose.*
4. *List any other goals you will be working on, any assigned building goal, or other goal assigned by your principal.*
5. *At the end of the year, note progress on goals.*
6. *Write down a possible goal for next year.*

Other Goals:

Progress on goals:

Possible goal for next year:

Resource Figure A.11.
Choice for Year 1 or 2: Standards-Based Goal

Evaluation Planning Worksheet
Growth-Focused Evaluation System

Teacher Name _____   **Date** _____

Selected Domain: _____
(From Professional Teaching Practice Domains)

First component: _____

Second component: _____

Questions about my teaching practice:

1. _____

2. _____

3. _____

Instrument(s) used _____

Resource Figure A.12.
Evaluation Planning Worksheet

Sample Evaluation Year 3 Questions About Teaching Practice; Domains and Components; Possible Data Collection Instruments

Sample Questions About Teaching Practice	Domain and Components	Possible Data Collection Instruments
1. Are my questioning and discussion techniques effective?	3—Instruction b. Using Questioning/Discussion	Media Recording, External Observer, Student Feedback
2. Do I group my students in ways that enhance instruction?	2—Classroom Environment c. Classroom Procedures	Media Recording, External Observer, Student Feedback
3. Do I manage transitions between lessons effectively?	3—Instruction c. Engaging Students	Media Recording, External Observer, Student Feedback
4. Do parents of my students feel sufficiently involved in their children's education?	4—Professional Responsibility c. Communicating With Families	Parent Feedback
5. Am I integrating the concept of multiple intelligences to the degree I'd like?	1—Planning and Preparation b. Demonstrating Knowledge of Students	Improvement Portfolio
6. Do my teaching methods target different ways of learning?	1—Planning and Preparation b. Demonstrating Knowledge of Students	Student Feedback, Improvement Portfolio
7. Do the assessment techniques I use reflect my beliefs about student learning?	3—Instruction d. Providing Feedback to Students	Improvement Portfolio, Student Feedback, Parent Feedback
8. Is the atmosphere in my classroom one that fosters respect and an easy rapport between the students as well as the students and myself?	2—Classroom Environment a. Respect and Rapport	Media Recording, Student Feedback
9. Have I made the best and safest use of my classroom and its contents, considering the changing needs of my students from one lesson to the next?	2—Classroom Environment e. Organizing Space	External Observer
10. How can I challenge all students? What resources are available? How are others coping with a wide range of academic needs?	1—Planning and Preparation c. Selecting Instructional Goals d. Demonstrating Knowledge of Resources	Improvement Portfolio, Student Performance Data, External Observer, Instruction-Based Project
11. How can I strengthen my reading instruction in the area of phonics from a strategic contextual perspective?	3—Instruction c. Engaging Students in Learning	External Observer, Instruction-Based Project
12. Do I communicate clearly with parents and students?	4—Professional Responsibility c. Communicating With Families	Parent Feedback, External Observer

Resource Figure A.13.
Professional Growth and Evaluation Process for the Experienced Teacher

Experienced Teachers' Sample Evaluation Instruments, Year 3

Type of Instrument	Title
External Observer	EO 1
	EO 2
	EO 3
	EO 4
Media Recording	MR 1
	MR 2
Student Feedback	SF 1
	SF 2
	SF 3
Parent Feedback	PF 1
	PF 2
Principal Observation (clinical supervision)	PO 1-A
	PO 1-B
	PO 1-C
Improvement Portfolio	IP
Instruction-Based Project	IBP

Resource Figure A.14.
Experienced Teachers' Sample Evaluation Instruments, Year 3

EXTERNAL OBSERVER #1
(EO 1)

Audience: Intended for use with teachers of Grades K-12; could be used by peers or administrators.

Action steps: Look for patterns of strengths and weaknesses in the lesson, as well as teaching patterns over several classes or a period of time. Check back to see whether improvements made as a result of first analysis have proved successful.

Analysis needed: A follow-up conversation must occur shortly after the observation. Observer and teacher write an analysis of lesson presented. Both analyses should include a discussion of possible future teaching practice changes.

Lesson Feedback

1. The best aspects of this lesson were:

2. The least successful aspects of this lesson were:

3. Improvements to the lesson could be:

4. A pattern noted across several classes, lessons, or weeks is:

Resource Figure A.15.
Year 3 Evaluation Instruments: External Observer #1 (EO 1)

Audience: Intended for use with teachers K-12; could be used with peers

Action steps: See below, collegial discussion

Analysis needed: Write an analysis of the substance of your conversation with
   your peer. Include a discussion of any action steps you will take as a result of
   this activity.

---

1. What is one teaching skill/strategy you would like to improve? Why?

2. Identify one or two teachers in this school or another that you respect and admire
   as colleagues from whom you could get helpful advice or whom you could observe
   so that you could improve the skill you have identified. (If you can't identify anyone, ask your principal or colleagues for assistance.)

3. Discuss the teaching skill/strategy you identified with the faculty member. You may
   also want to observe that person use this skill in action and/or have him or her observe you to coach you as you try to implement and practice this skill/strategy.

4. Write an analysis of this process, reflecting on your learning, and state your future
   action plan.

SOURCE: Adapted from *Teacher Self-Evaluation Tool Kit*, by P. W. Airasian and A. R. Gullickson, 1997,
Thousand Oaks, CA: Corwin.

Resource Figure A.16.
Year 3 Evaluation Instruments: External Observer #2 (EO 2)

Audience: Intended for use with teachers K-12; could be used by peers or administrators. Focus is on teacher and student discourse.

Action steps: Use the data collected to answer the questions asked.

Analysis needed: A follow-up conversation must occur shortly after the observation. Observer and teacher write an analysis of the data collected. Both analyses should include a discussion of possible future changes in teaching practice.

1. What are several questions you have about the nature and content of classroom discussion in your room? For example, what proportion of time is spent in teacher talk? How many students participate in discussion? How much time is spent responding to student questions? How much time is spent on lesson setup and purpose? State your questions below:

2. Jot down short answers to the questions stated above. Do this before observation.

3. After the observation, complete an analysis by comparing the preobservation answers you wrote with the postobservation data.

SOURCE: Adapted from *Teacher Self-Evaluation Tool Kit,* by P. W. Airasian and A. R. Gullickson, 1997, Thousand Oaks, CA: Corwin.

Resource Figure A.17.
Year 3 Evaluation Instruments: External Observer #3 (EO 3)

Audience: Intended for use with teachers K-12; could be used by peers or administrators. Focus is on teacher feedback to students.

Action steps: Use the data collected to answer the questions asked.

Analysis needed: A follow-up conversation must occur shortly after the observation. Observer and teacher write an analysis of the data collected. Both analyses should include a discussion of possible future changes in teaching practice.

---

1. Consider the following questions about your feedback to students:

   - How soon do I provide feedback on student work and ideas?
   - How specific is the feedback? Do I use vague or general feedback like "good," "poor vocabulary," or "work on this"? Or do I use specific feedback that informs the student, like "good combination of adjectives to convey meaning"?
   - Do I focus feedback on specific behaviors that students can work on?
   - Do I show students how to perform correctly or give them examples of good performance?
   - Do I try to balance negative feedback with positive feedback?
   - Do I try to teach students to judge their own performance? Do I give them guidance in doing this?

List below any other questions you may have about student feedback:

2. After the observation, complete an analysis by comparing your preobservation perceptions and concerns with the postobservation data.

SOURCE: Adapted from *Teacher Self-Evaluation Tool Kit*, by P. W. Airasian and A. R. Gullickson, 1997, Thousand Oaks, CA: Corwin.

Resource Figure A.18.
Year 3 Evaluation Instruments: External Observer #4 (EO 4)

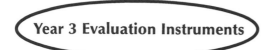

MEDIA RECORDING #1
(MR 1)

Audience: Intended for use with teachers K-12; could be used by peers or administrators. Focus is on teacher feedback to students collected by means of tape or video recording.

Action steps: Use the data collected to answer the questions asked.

Analysis needed: A follow-up conversation and review of the tape must occur shortly after the observation. Teacher (and observer, if applicable) write an analysis of the data collected. Analysis should include a discussion of possible future changes in teaching practice.

---

1. Consider the following questions about your feedback to students:

   - How soon do I provide feedback on student work and ideas?

   - How specific is the feedback? Do I use vague or general feedback like "good," "poor vocabulary," or "work on this"? Or do I use specific feedback that informs the student, like "good combination of adjectives to convey meaning"?

   - Do I focus feedback on specific behaviors students can work on?

   - Do I show students how to perform correctly or give them examples of good performance?

   - Do I try to balance negative feedback with positive feedback?

   - Do I try to teach students to judge their own performance? Do I give them guidance in doing this?

List below any other questions you may have about student feedback:

2. After the observation, complete an analysis by comparing your preobservation perceptions and concerns with the postobservation data.

SOURCE: Adapted from *Teacher Self-Evaluation Tool Kit*, by P. W. Airasian and A. R. Gullickson, 1997, Thousand Oaks, CA: Corwin.

Resource Figure A.19.
Year 3 Evaluation Instruments: Media Recording #1 (MR 1)

Year 3 Evaluation Instruments

MEDIA RECORDING #2
(MR 2)

Audience: Intended for use with teachers K-12; could be used by peers or administrators. Focus is on teacher and student discourse collected by means of tape or video recording.

Action steps: Use the data collected to answer the questions asked.

Analysis needed: A follow-up conversation and review of the tape must occur shortly after the observation. Teacher (and observer, if applicable) write an analysis of the data collected. Analysis should include a discussion of possible future changes in teaching practice.

---

1. What are several questions you have about the nature and content of classroom discussion in your room? For example, what proportion of time is spent in teacher talk? How many students participate in discussion? How much time is spent responding to student questions? How much time is spent on lesson setup and purpose? State your questions below:

2. Jot down short answers to the questions stated above. Do this before observation.

3. After the observation, complete an analysis by comparing the preobservation answers you wrote with the postobservation data.

SOURCE: Adapted from *Teacher Self-Evaluation Tool Kit*, by P. W. Airasian and A. R. Gullickson, 1997, Thousand Oaks, CA: Corwin.

Resource Figure A.20.
Year 3 Evaluation Instruments: Media Recording #2 (MR 2)

STUDENT FEEDBACK #1
(SF 1)

Audience: Intended for use with teachers 4-12; could be used by administrators. Focus is on student feedback about a particular unit, activity, or yearlong experience with the teacher.

Action steps: Compose a survey or use the sample below and collect data from students.

Analysis needed: Write an analysis of the data you collected. Analysis should include a discussion of possible future changes in teaching practice.

1. In what areas would you would like student feedback? These areas could relate to a specific project or activity, a certain instructional approach, assessment practices, or other teacher characteristics. Develop questions about these areas.

2. Predict student responses to your questions before reading the actual student responses.

3. Ask students to respond to the questions anonymously in writing.

4. Identify needed changes and develop an action plan to implement the changes in your classroom.

SOURCE: Adapted from *Teacher Self-Evaluation Tool Kit,* by P. W. Airasian and A. R. Gullickson, 1997, Thousand Oaks, CA: Corwin.

Resource Figure A.21.
Year 3 Evaluation Instruments: Student Feedback #1 (SF 1)

STUDENT FEEDBACK #2
(SF 2)

Audience: Intended for use with teachers of Grades 2-12; could be used by administrators. Focus is on student feedback about the learning environment.

Action steps: Compose a survey or use the sample below and collect data from students. Surveys should not be signed by students, but done anonymously.

Analysis needed: Write an analysis of the data you collected. Analysis should include a discussion of possible future changes in teaching practice.

Circle the best answer to each question listed below:

1. My teacher encourages me to do my best.   Yes   No   Sometimes

2. My teacher uses many different ways to teach us.   Yes   No   Sometimes

3. We have good rules in our class.   Yes   No   Sometimes

4. Students work together well in the classroom.   Yes   No   Sometimes

5. My teacher tries to live out in actions what he or she says.   Yes   No   Sometimes

6. We have interesting class discussions.   Yes   No   Sometimes

7. My teacher cares about me as a person.   Yes   No   Sometimes

8. I can see that my teacher gets excited about teaching.   Yes   No   Sometimes

Resource Figure A.22.
Year 3 Evaluation Instruments: Student Feedback #2 (SF 2)

STUDENT FEEDBACK #3
(SF 3)

> **Audience:** Intended for use with teachers of grades 6-12, could be used by administrators. Focus is on student feedback about the learning environment and teacher qualities.
>
> **Action steps:** Compose a survey or use the sample below and collect data from students. Surveys should not be signed by students, but done anonymously.
>
> **Analysis needed:** Write an analysis of the data you collected. Analysis should include a discussion of possible future changes in teaching practice.

Write a short answer for each question.

1. What kind of feedback from me helped the most in improving your performance?

2. What aspects of this class were the most frustrating to you?

3. Were the content and activities in this class stimulating to you? Why or why not?

4. Did this class function as a community of people who worked well together? Why or why not?

5. What advice would you give to someone assigned to this class next semester or next year?

6. What positive changes can you suggest to improve this class? My teaching?

Resource Figure A.23.
Year 3 Evaluation Instruments: Student Feedback #3 (SF 3)

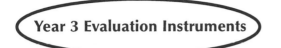

PARENT FEEDBACK #1
(PF 1)

> **Audience:** Intended for use with teachers of Grades K-12; could be used by admin-istrators. Focus is on receiving feedback from current and former parents on issues relevant to the teacher.
>
> **Action steps:** See steps outlined below.
>
> **Analysis needed:** Write an analysis of the data you collected. Analysis should include a discussion of possible future changes in teaching practice.

Action Steps for Parent Survey

1. Determine the issues or items on which you would like feedback from parents.
2. Design a survey to address the identified issues. Show a copy of the survey to the principal prior to distribution to parents.
3. Distribute the survey to:
   a. all the parents of current students in the class from which you would like feedback.
   b. half of the parents of students from the relevant class 2 years prior identified at random.
4. Identify on the survey or cover letter that (a) the surveys are to be returned to the principal and (b) you as teacher will be reading the responses. Signatures by respon-dents are optional. (The principal and the teacher should discuss in advance at what time, if any, the principal will read the surveys.)
5. Give parents at least 2 weeks to respond to the survey.
6. Retrieve surveys from the principal at the end of 2 weeks. The total and actual sam-ple size should be taken into consideration when determining the relevance of the surveys.
7. After reading the survey results, write an analysis of the responses to the identified issues in Step 1. Include a statement of what you have learned from the surveys and what effect that learning will have on your work.
8. Meet with your principal to discuss the results.

Resource Figure A.24.
Year 3 Evaluation Instruments: Parent Feedback #1 (PF 1)

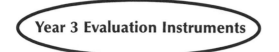

Audience: Intended for use with teachers of grades K-8; could be used by administrators. Focus is on receiving feedback from current and former parents on issues relevant to the teacher.

Action steps: See Form PF 1 for instructions.

Analysis needed: Write an analysis of the data you collected. Analysis should include a discussion of possible future changes in teaching practice.

Parent Survey

Date_____   Name (optional)_____

4 = Strongly agree   3 = Agree   2 = Disagree   1 = Strongly disagree   0 = Not applicable (N/A)

1. Is your child's attitude favorable about school in general this year?   4 3 2 1 0

2. Do I communicate effectively with you in oral or written form?   4 3 2 1 0

3. Do I communicate expectations clearly to your child?   4 3 2 1 0

4. Are the class assignments, projects, and workload age/grade appropriate?   4 3 2 1 0

5. Do I deal fairly and consistently with behavioral issues?   4 3 2 1 0

6. Do I communicate a caring and positive attitude to your child?   4 3 2 1 0

7. Do I encourage your child's participation and learning?   4 3 2 1 0

8. Have you have felt welcome in your child's classroom?   4 3 2 1 0

Comments:

Please return this survey by (date) to the building principal's office. Thank you!

Resource Figure A.25.
Year 3 Evaluation Instruments: Parent Feedback #2 (PF 2)

PRINCIPAL OBSERVATION
(PO 1-A)

Audience: Intended for use with teachers of Grades K-12; intended for use by administrators.

Action steps: Follow clinical supervision cycle; follow steps listed below.

Analysis needed: Write an analysis of the data you collected. Analysis should include a discussion of possible future changes in teaching practice.

Principal Observation Steps Using the Clinical Supervision Model

1. Teacher should complete Form PO 1-B (Principal Observation, Preobservation Questions) and Form PO 1-C (Principal Observation, Instructional Focus), which immediately follow this page.
2. Teacher should schedule a meeting with the principal to discuss the above two forms. Principal and teacher should agree on the focus of the observation, the instrument to be used, and the time of the observation.
3. Observation takes place.
4. A postconference is held within 48 hours regarding the results of the observation. Principal will give a copy of the notes taken during the observation to the teacher immediately following the observation for the teacher's reflection before the postconference.

Resource Figure A.26.
Year 3 Evaluation Instruments: Principal Observation (PO 1-A)

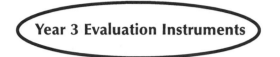

PRINCIPAL OBSERVATION
(PO 1-B)
(Preobservation Questions)

Teacher _____ Class _____ Date_____

1. Where are you in the course (e.g., unit, lesson, page numbers)?

2. What teaching/learning activities will be observed?

3. What skills, attitudes, understandings will be taught? (What are your students going to get out of it?)

4. How are you going to do it? What methods you will use?

5. What, if any, particular teaching behaviors do you especially want monitored?

6. How are you going to know whether the students have learned?

7. What special characteristics/needs of the students should be noted?

8. Anything else we need to discuss?

Resource Figure A.27.
Year 3 Evaluation Instruments: Principal Observation (PO 1-B)

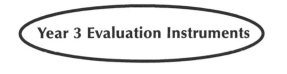

Year 3 Evaluation Instruments

PRINCIPAL OBSERVATION
(PO 1-C)
(Instructional Focus)

Teacher _____ **Class** _____ **Date**_____

Given the focus of the instruction in the lesson and the goals of this observation, what type of observation instrument would best help collect the needed data?

1. *Selective verbatim:* Written record of selected verbal events

2. *Teacher questions:* Written record of questions asked by teacher

3. *Teacher feedback:* Written record of teacher feedback statements to students

4. *Teacher directions and structuring statements:* Written record of the amount, variety, and specificity of directions and structuring statements

5. *Anecdotal records:* Objective notes of classroom interaction and events, looking at the "big picture"

Resource Figure A.28.
Year 3 Evaluation Instruments: Principal Observation (PO 1-C)

Audience: Intended for use by teachers of Grades K-12. Focus is on change or improvement of a particular teaching area or skill through analysis of several performances.

Action steps: Compile information for your portfolio.

Analysis needed: Write an analysis of your improvement as a teacher. Analysis should include a discussion of possible future changes in teaching practice.

The goal of the portfolio is to document change and improvement in one's teaching performance over a period of time.

Many of the previous tools in this section could be applied and repeated several times during a year or years to note improvement in a specific area. Many areas of focus are possible for portfolio self-evaluation. One example is given below to demonstrate how it actually might occur.

Example:

Choice of instrument: External observer

Instructional focus: Questioning strategies with students

Cycle: Observation, conversation with observer, analysis, plans for change, implementation of change, second observation, conversation, analysis, possible third observation, and so on.

Analysis through the portfolio: Have I improved my teaching practice? Have I correctly identified areas of weakness and strength? Have the changes I made to my practice been effective and maintainable? How can I continue to build on what I have learned and implemented?

SOURCE: Adapted from *Teacher Self-Evaluation Tool Kit,* by P. W. Airasian and A. R. Gullickson, 1997, Thousand Oaks, CA: Corwin.

Resource Figure A.29.
Year 3 Evaluation Instruments: Improvement Portfolio (IP)

INSTRUCTION-BASED PROJECT
(IBP)

Audience: Intended for use by teachers of Grades K-12. Focus is on change or improvement of instruction through development of more effective and meaningful teaching/learning experiences or materials for students (hereafter called project, for ease of reference).

Action steps: Analyze current teaching practice to determine areas of needed improvement. Identify the type of change needed for more effective student learning to occur. Discuss the idea for change with your supervisor and arrive at a mutually agreeable plan of action to develop and implement the project.

Analysis needed: Write an analysis of how the project you developed as a teacher has affected student learning. Include reflections on your own growth as you went through the process of developing the project. How will you assess the effectiveness of the project you developed? Analysis should include a discussion of possible future changes in teaching practice.

Name_____ **Date** _____

Area of instructional practice I'd like to improve:

Proposed project to improve student learning:

I will know the project is a success with students by:

Resource Figure A.30.
Year 3 Evaluation Instruments: Instruction-Based Project (IBP)

Professional Growth and Evaluation Process
for the Beginning Teacher

Beginning teachers are defined as follows:

Beginning—no prior teaching experience

Transfer to system—an experienced teacher who has transferred to the system

Expectations for evaluation of the beginning teacher

Classroom observations will be made according to the following schedule:

Year 1. Minimum of two formal written observations during the first semester and one in the second semester. Administrators may make several informal visits during the first 2 months of school to ensure that everything is going smoothly.

Year 2. Minimum of two formal written observations during the first semester and one in the second semester.

Year 3. If satisfactory evaluations have been recorded in the first 2 years, the teacher may be moved into the experienced teacher 3-year cycle.

Expectations for evaluation of the transferring experienced teacher

Years 1 and 2. Minimum of two formal observations by the administrator using the clinical supervision process

Year 3. If satisfactory evaluations have been recorded in the first 2 years, the teacher may be moved into the experienced teacher 3-year cycle.

Nonrenewal of contract

Nonrenewal decisions may be based on evaluations, enrollment, or budgetary constraints. If evaluations indicate unsatisfactory performance, then the teacher should be assisted according to the RISC plan or terminated. Notification of termination will be given by February 1, and an appeal to the superintendent may be made by March 1.

Resource Figure A.31.
Professional Growth and Evaluation Process for the Beginning Teacher

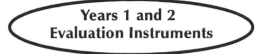

PRINCIPAL OBSERVATION
(PO 1-A)

> **Audience:** Intended for use with teachers of Grades K-12; intended for use by administrators.
>
> **Action steps:** Follow clinical supervision cycle; follow steps listed below.
>
> **Analysis needed:** Write an analysis of the data you collected. Analysis should include a discussion of possible future changes in teaching practice.

Principal Observation Steps Using the Clinical Supervision Model

1. Teacher should complete Form PO 1-B (Principal Observation, Preobservation Questions) and Form PO 1-C (Principal Observation, Instructional Focus), which immediately follow this page.

2. Teacher should schedule a meeting with principal to discuss the above two forms. Principal and teacher should agree on the focus of the observation, the instrument to be used, and the time of the observation.

3. Observation takes place.

4. A postconference is held within 48 hours regarding the results of the observation. Principal will give a copy of the notes taken during the observation to the teacher immediately following the observation for the teacher's reflection before the postconference.

Resource Figure A.32.
Years 1 and 2 Evaluation Instruments: Principal Observation (PO 1-A)

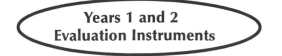

Teacher _____ **Class**_____ **Date**_____

1. Where are you in the course (e.g., unit, lesson, page numbers)?

2. What teaching/learning activities will be observed?

3. What skills, attitudes, understandings will be taught? (What are your students going to get out of it?)

4. How are you going to do it? What methods you will use?

5. What, if any, particular teaching behaviors do you especially want monitored?

6. How are you going to know whether the students have learned?

7. What special characteristics/needs of the students should be noted?

8. Anything else we need to discuss?

Resource Figure A.33.
Years 1 and 2 Evaluation Instruments: Principal Observation (PO 1-B)

**Years 1 and 2
Evaluation Instruments**

**PRINCIPAL OBSERVATION
(PO 1-C)
(Instructional Focus)**

Teacher _____ **Class**_____ **Date**_____

Given the focus of the instruction in the lesson and the goals of this observation, what type of observation instrument would best help collect the needed data?

1. *Selective verbatim:* Written record of selected verbal events

2. *Teacher questions:* Written record of questions asked by teacher

3. *Teacher feedback:* Written record of teacher feedback statements to students

4. *Teacher directions and structuring statements:* Written record of the amount, variety, and specificity of directions and structuring statements

5. *Anecdotal records:* Objective notes of classroom interaction and events, looking at the "big picture"

Resource Figure A.34.
Years 1 and 2 Evaluation Instruments: Principal Observation (PO 1-C)

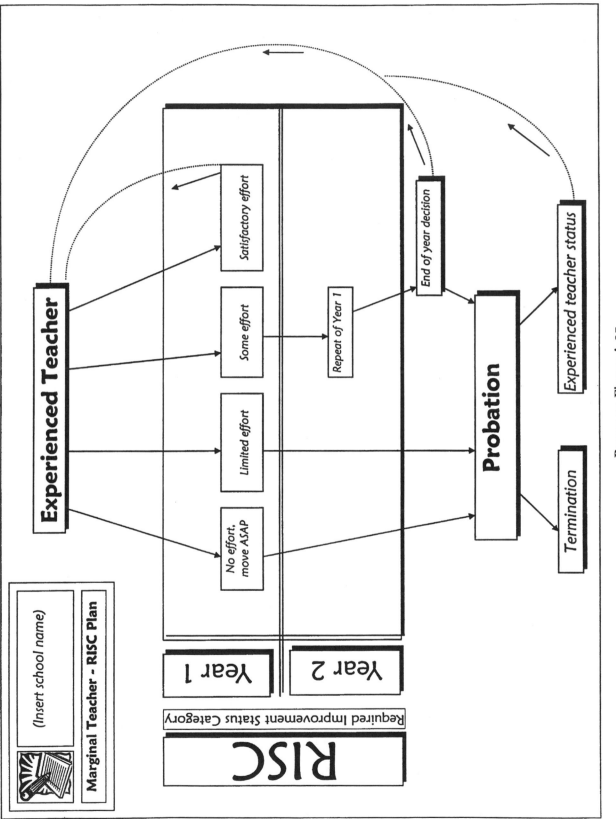

Resource Figure A.35.
Marginal Teacher—RISC Plan

146

Professional Growth and Evaluation Process
for the Marginal Teacher

1. When an experienced teacher is demonstrating insufficient growth or serious deficiencies in her or his professional practice she or he will be placed in RISC
(required improvement status category). RISC is designed to be a period of intensive
assistance for the experienced teacher. Significant effort must be demonstrated by
the teacher to show improvement. Administration also provides significant assistance and support to the teacher to aid in the improvement process.

2. RISC is a maximum 2-year process. Teacher placement decisions will be made by
administration in communication with the Education Committee.

3. When placed in RISC, four categories are possible, and placement into a category is
dependent on teacher response and growth as determined by administration:

    a. Teacher shows no effort and does not respond to, or resists remediation—moved
    immediately into the probation process, or in extreme cases terminated as soon
    as possible. Typically, this decision must be made in September or October so
    that appropriate measures can be taken and due process can be followed.

    b. Teacher shows limited effort toward remediation of problem areas. After Year 1,
    the decision would be to give the teacher a probationary year contract.

    c. Teacher shows some effort toward remediation of problem areas. The decision at
    the end of the year would be to have the teacher continue in a second year of
    RISC, receiving intensive remediation. At the end of Year 2, a decision would be
    made whether the teacher has made significant enough improvement to return to
    the experienced teacher category or whether she or he would enter probation
    year status.

    d. Teacher shows satisfactory improvement in identified problem areas and after
    1 year can be returned to the experienced teacher category.

4. Teachers placed on probation will follow the process laid out on the following
pages. *Probation* is a period of intensive assistance and due process in a last attempt
to assist the teacher to reach a satisfactory level of performance. This period is not
to exceed 1 year; typically, the teacher who begins the year in probation may receive notice of intention of termination by January if progress is not demonstrated.
Teachers who demonstrate significant and satisfactory improvement may be
returned to the experienced teacher category.

Resource Figure A.36.
Professional Growth and Evaluation Process for the Marginal Teacher

**Professional Growth and Evaluation Process
for the Probationary Teacher**

1. The process of probation is a period of intensive assistance and due process in a final attempt to assist the teacher to reach a satisfactory level of performance and/or conduct. This period is not to exceed 1 year; typically, the teacher who begins the year in probation will receive notice of intention of termination by January if sufficient progress is not demonstrated. Teachers who demonstrate significant and satisfactory improvement may be returned to the experienced teacher category. The process for teachers and administrators to follow in a probationary year is listed below.

2. The teacher will be notified of probationary status. The building administrator will review recommendations for improvement with the teacher at the appropriate time and provide assistance plans. Most often, this will occur at the beginning of the year when a teacher has been in the RISC category the year before. In more severe cases, however, the process may be accelerated and take place at any time in the year. An accelerated process will follow similar steps as listed below except on an accelerated time frame.

3. A probationary teacher's intensive assistance plans may include (a) observation of another teacher for a day in the same school and another school for a day, (b) assistance by another teacher for a day in the probationary teacher's classroom, (c) attendance at appropriate workshops, (d) helpful articles and videos, and (e) recommendations from administrator observations.

4. Administrators will conduct a minimum of two classroom observations per month during the months of September through December, using the clinical supervision model. These observations will include identified areas of weakness and recommendations for improvement and state a reasonable amount of time for improvement. Administrators involved in the observations will include the building principal and other qualified designees. Part of the observation process may include collecting from the teacher samples of assignments given to students and discipline referral records.

5. If a teacher's performance does not improve, he or she will receive a letter in December, stating the possibility of an unsatisfactory final evaluation with recommendation for dismissal if his or her performance does not improve by January 15.

6. An unsatisfactory final evaluation meeting will be conducted in January with the teacher and the Education Committee of the school board. If the Education Committee approves the termination of the contract, this will take the form of a recommendation to the school board.

7. The school board will act on the recommendation, and its decision will be considered final.

Resource Figure A.37.
Professional Growth and Evaluation Process for the Probationary Teacher

Guidelines for Termination of Contract

1. Grounds for termination must be put in writing by the principal and other evaluators and be presented to the staff member, Education Committee, superintendent, and school board.

2. The staff member will be granted a hearing before each authority dealing with the matter (Education Committee and school board) and will be given adequate notice of times of all meetings.

3. Both the staff member and the authority dealing with the matter may have a counselor present.

4. Each authority dealing with the matter must act promptly and present its decision in writing to the staff member involved.

SOURCE: A primary reference for the process above and the sample documents was *The Marginal Teacher: A Step-by-Step Guide to Fair Procedures for Identification and Dismissal,* by C. E. Lawrence, M. K. Vachon, D. O. Leake, and B. H. Leake, 1993, Newbury Park, CA: Corwin.

Resource Figure A.37.
Continued

Memorandum

To: Professional Growth Year Teachers
From: Dan
Date: October 1, 1999
Re: Goal setting for professional growth

Please review the following sections in the *Growth-Focused Evaluation System* (GFES) notebook:

Teacher Professional Growth Years 1 & 2

After reflection, select one of two categories: Big Picture Option or Standards-Based Goals. (You will work in the other area next year.)

Once you have selected a category, choose from the three activities listed under the title. Follow the steps listed under that activity as you work on your goal.

It is also appropriate to follow up on a previous year's goal. Please recall that I am assigning everyone one goal that we have already discussed: Complete the technology staff development checklist and review it with our tech coordinator. I have attached a copy of the checklist to this memo. Please list this goal on the Professional Growth Worksheet too.

Please make an appointment with me soon to review the goals that you have selected. You should come to the conference with the goals articulated on the Professional Growth Worksheet (also attached.) If you have any questions, I would be happy to help you in any way.

Thanks for your attention to this matter.

Resource Figure A.38.
Sample Administrative Memo for Professional Growth Year Teachers

Memorandum

To: Evaluation Year Teachers
From: Dan
Date: October 1, 1999
Re: Evaluation process

During the evaluation year, the focus is on teaching practice as summarized in the Professional Teaching Practice Domains area. Please familiarize yourself with this section of the GFES notebook. Use the Evaluation Planning Worksheet (attached) to guide you as you select an area of focus in examining your practice.

First, select a domain from the four. Second, select two components from this domain. Next, formulate two or three questions about your practice as it relates to these components (see the sheet Sample Evaluation Year 3 Questions About Teaching Practice; Domains and Components; Possible Data Collection Instrument). For example, if you had selected Component 3d, Providing Feedback to Students, your question might be "Is my feedback timely, accurate, constructive, and specific?" To obtain data for answering your question, look at the Experienced Teachers' Sample Evaluation Instruments, Year 3 chart to select an instrument. Two instruments (there may be others) that could help you answer the question would be (a) have an observer in your classroom or (b) videotape yourself. You would list this on the last line of the Evaluation Planning Worksheet under "Instrument(s) used."

After you have completed the worksheet or if you have further questions, please set a time to review it with me at your earliest convenience.

Resource Figure A.39.
Sample Administrative Memo for Evaluation Year Teachers

Probationary Teacher Observation Record

Teacher _____ Date _____ Observer _____

Concern	Suggestion	Timeframe

Resource Figure A.40.
Probationary Teacher Observation Record

Professional Growth and Evaluation Faculty Summary

School _____

Year _____

Resource Figure A.41.
Professional Growth and Evaluation Faculty Summary

Name	Big Picture Options			Standards Based Goal			Goals
	TE	*RG TP*	*C& LD*	*NG*	*IG*	*IB Pr*	*(State main goal set for the year)*

TE = Topic Exploration	NG = New Goal
RG = Reflection on General Teaching Practice	IG = Identified Goal during previous year
C&LD = Career and Leadership Development	IB Pr = Instruction-based project

Resource Figure A.42.
Years 1 & 2 Professional Growth Teacher Summary
Growth-Focused Evaluation System
(for administrative use)

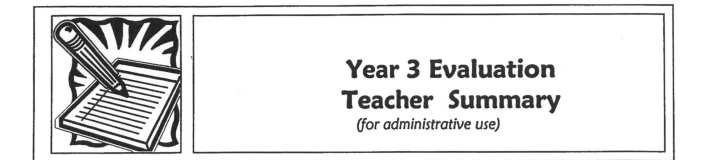

Name	*Domain*	Comp. 1	Comp. 2	Questions Asked Re: Practice

Resource Figure A.43.
Year 3 Evaluation Teacher Summary

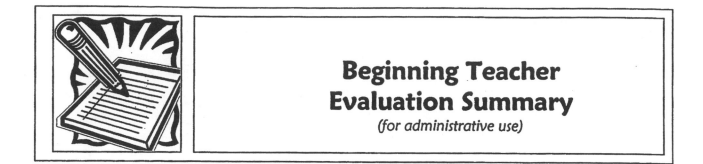

Beginning Teacher Evaluation Summary
(for administrative use)

Name	Dates Observed	Progress Noted

Resource Figure A.44.
Beginning Teacher Evaluation Summary

Marginal Teacher
Evaluation Summary

Name	Dates Observed	Progress Noted and Recommendation for Action

Resource Figure A.45.
Marginal Teacher Evaluation Summary

References

Acheson, K., & Gall, M. (1987). *Techniques in the clinical supervision of teachers* (2nd ed.). White Plains, NY: Longman.

Airasian, P. W. (1995, January). *Teacher self-evaluation tool kit.* Draft of a paper prepared for the Hawaii Institute on Assessment and Accountability, Hawaii Department of Education, Honolulu.

Airasian, P. W., & Gullickson, A. R. (1994). Examination of teacher self-assessment. *Journal of Personnel Evaluation in Education, 8,* 195-203.

Airasian, P. W., & Gullickson, A. R. (1997). *Teacher self-evaluation tool kit.* Thousand Oaks, CA: Corwin.

Allen, D. W., Nichols, R. D., & Leblanc, A. C. (1997). The prime teacher appraisal program: 2+2 for teachers. *High School Magazine, 4*(4), 30-35.

Archer, J. (1998a). Students' fortunes rest with assigned teacher. *Education Week, 17,* 3.

Archer, J. (1998b). In survey of 622 superintendents, U.S. schools earn a B. *Education Week, 18*(8), 11.

Blanchard, K., Zigarmi, P., & Zigarmi, D. (1985). *Leadership and the one minute manager.* New York: Morrow.

Bolman, L. G., & Deal, T. E. (1995). *Leading with soul: An uncommon journey of spirit.* San Francisco: Jossey-Bass.

Boyd, R. (1989). *Improving teacher evaluations.* (ERIC Document Reproduction Service No. ED 315 431)

Chase, B. (1997). Teacher vs. teacher? Nonsense. *Education Week, 17,* 26-29.

Cornett, L. M. (1995). Lessons from 10 years of teacher improvement reforms. *Educational Leadership, 52,* 26-30.

Costa, A. L., & Garmston, R. (1985). Supervision for intelligent teaching. *Educational Leadership, 42,* 70-80.

Covey, S. (1991). *Principle-centered leadership.* New York: Summit.

Danielson, C. (1996). *Enhancing professional practice: A framework for teaching.* Alexandria, VA: Association for Supervision and Curriculum Development.

Darling-Hammond, L. (1997). Quality teaching: The critical key to learning [On-line]. Available: http://www.naesp.org/comm/ p0997a.htm

Darling-Hammond, L., & Sclan, E. (1992). Policy and supervision. In C. D. Glickman (Ed.), *Supervision in transition: 1992 yearbook of* the Association for Supervision and Curriculum Development (pp. 7-29). Alexandria, VA: Association for Supervision and Curriculum Development.

DePree, M. (1989). *Leadership is an art.* New York: Dell.

DePree, M. (1992). *Leadership jazz.* Garden City, NY: Doubleday.

Doolittle, P. (1994). *Teacher portfolio assessment.* (ERIC Document Reproduction Service No. ED 385 608)

Doud, J. L., & Keller, E. P. (1998). The K-8 principal in 1998 [On-line]. Available: http://www.naesp.org/comm/p0998d.htm

Drucker, P. F. (1998). Management's new paradigms. *Forbes, 162*(7), 152-176.

Education Week on the Web. Quality counts '98 [On-line]. Available: http://www.naesp.org/comm/p0998d.htm

Farson, R. (1996). *Management of the absurd: Paradoxes in leadership.* New York: Simon & Schuster.

Glasser, W. (1992). *The quality school: Managing students without coercion* (2nd ed.). New York: HarperCollins.

Glasser, W. (1993). *The quality school teacher.* New York: HarperCollins.

Glatthorn, A. A., & Coble, C. R. (1995). What to do about teacher quality: Don't eliminate tenure, there is a better route to improving the corps. *Education Week, 14*, 35-38.

Glickman, C. D. (Ed.). (1992). *Supervision in transition: 1992 yearbook of the Association for Supervision and Curriculum Development.* Alexandria, VA: Association for Supervision and Curriculum Development.

Goleman, D. (1995). *Emotional intelligence.* New York: Bantam.

Goleman, D. (1998). *Working with emotional intelligence.* New York: Bantam.

Harrington-Leuker, D. (1996). Chuck the checklist. *Executive Educator, 18*(6), 21-24.

Hoerr, T. R. (1996). Collegiality: A new way to define instructional leadership. *Phi Delta Kappan, 77*(5), 380-381.

Holt, M. (1993). Deming on education: A view from the seminar. *Phi Delta Kappan, 75*(4), 329-330.

Johnston, R. C. (1999). Reform bills pass in California legislature. *Education Week, 18*, 1, 18.

Jones, R. (1997). Showing bad teachers the door. *American School Board Journal, 184*, 21-24.

Keller, B. (1997). Seattle teachers approve tentative contract with broad new evaluation, hiring policies. *Education Week, 17*, 8.

Keller, B. (1998). Principal matters. *Education Week, 18*(11), 25-27.

Knoke, W. (1996). *Bold new world: The essential road map to the 21st century.* New York: Kodansha America.

Krovetz, M., & Cohick, D. (1993). Professional collegiality can lead to school change. *Phi Delta Kappan, 75*(4), 331-333.

Lambert, L. (1998). *Building leadership capacity in schools.* Alexandria, VA: Association for Supervision and Curriculum Development.

Lawrence, C. E., Vachon, M. K., Leake, D. O., & Leake, B. H. (1993). *The marginal teacher: A step-by-step guide to fair procedures for identification and dismissal.* Newbury Park, CA: Corwin.

Lawton, M. (1997). Parents in N.Y. district to critique teachers. *Education Week, 17,* 3.

Lezotte, L. W. (1993). Creating the total quality effective school. *Book Summaries for Educators, 8-B,* 1-8.

Lieberman, A. (1995). Practices that support teacher development: Transforming conceptions of professional learning. *Phi Delta Kappan, 76*(8), 591-596.

Manatt, R. P. (1997). Feedback from 360 degrees: Client-driven evaluation of school personnel. *School Administrator, 54*(3), 8-13.

Marshall, K. (1996). How I confronted HSPS (hyperactive superficial principal syndrome) and began to deal with the heart of the matter. *Phi Delta Kappan, 77*(5), 336-345.

Mayo, R. W. (1997). Trends in teacher evaluation. *Clearing House, 70*(5), 269-272.

McCloskey, W., & Egelson, P. (1993). *Designing teacher evaluation systems that support professional growth.* Greensboro: University of North Carolina, Southeastern Regional Vision for Education.

McGreal, T. L. (1993, December). *Redesigning your teacher evaluation system.* Paper presented at the Michigan Institute for Educational Management.

Medley, D. M., Coker, H., & Soar, R. S. (1984). *Measurement-based evaluation of teacher performance: An empirical approach.* White Plains, NY: Longman.

Miller, J. A. (1998). State policy update [On-line]. Available: http://www.edweek.org/sreports/qc98/states/

Nolan, J., & Francis, P. (1992). Changing perspective in curriculum and instruction. In C. D. Glickman (Ed.), *Supervision in transition: 1992 yearbook of the Association for Supervision and Curriculum Development* (pp. 44-60). Alexandria, VA: Association for Supervision and Curriculum Development.

O'Neil, J. (1993). Supervision reappraised. *ASCD Update, 35*(6), 1-8.

Patterson, J. L. (1993). *Leadership for tomorrow's schools.* Alexandria, VA: Association for Supervision and Curriculum Development.

Perkins, D. (1992). *Smart schools: From training memories to educating minds.* New York: Free Press.

Peterson, K. D. (1995). *Teacher evaluation: A comprehensive guide to new directions and practices.* Thousand Oaks, CA: Corwin.

Peterson, K. D., Stevens, D., & Ponzio, R. C. (1998). Variable data sources in teacher evaluation. *Journal of Research and Development in Education, 31*(3), 123-132.

Ponticell, J. A. (1995). Promoting teacher professionalism through collegiality. *Journal of Staff Development, 16*(3), 13-17.

Quinn, T. (1998, Fall). A differentiated model of professional development. *ASCD Professional Development Newsletter,* pp. 1-6.

Reitzug, U. C., & Burrello, L. C. (1995). How principals can build self-renewing schools. *Educational Leadership, 52,* 48-50.

Renyi, J. (1998). Building learning into the teaching job. *Educational Leadership, 55*(5), 70-74.

Sanders, W. L. (1998). Value-added assessment. *School Administrator, 55*(11) [On-line]. Available: http://www.aasa.org/SchoolAdmin/dec9801.htm

Saphier, J., & Gower, R. (1997). *The skillful teacher: Building your teaching skills* (5th ed.). Carlisle, MA: Research for Better Teaching.

Sava, S. G. (1998). The name of the game [On-line]. Available: http://www.naesp.org/comm/p0998c.htm

Schlechty, P. C. (1990). *Schools for the 21st century: Leadership imperatives for educational reform.* San Francisco: Jossey-Bass.

Schmoker, M. (1996). *Results: The key to continuous school improvement.* Alexandria, VA: Association for Supervision and Curriculum Development.

Schrag, F. (1995). Teacher accountability: A philosophical view. *Phi Delta Kappan, 76*(8), 642-644.

Sergiovanni, T. J. (1992). *Moral leadership: Getting to the heart of school improvement.* San Francisco: Jossey-Bass.

Showers, B., & Joyce, B. (1996). The evolution of peer coaching. *Educational Leadership, 53,* 12-16.

Slater, R. (1999). *Jack Welch and the GE way: Management insights and leadership secrets of the legendary CEO.* New York: McGraw-Hill.

Sparks, D. (1997). A new vision for staff development. *Principal, 77,* 20-22.

Sparks, D., & Hirsch, S. (1997). *A new vision for staff development.* Alexandria, VA: Association for Supervision and Curriculum Development.

Stanley, S. J., & Popham, W. J. (Eds.). (1988). *Teacher evaluation: Six prescriptions for success.* Alexandria, VA: Association for Supervision and Curriculum Development.

Urbanski, A. (1997). Should parents evaluate our professional skills? *American Teacher, 82*(3), 4.

Van Wagenen, L., & Hibbard, M. (1998). Building teacher portfolios. *Educational Leadership, 55,* 26-29.

Willis, S. (1998). The public's priorities for improving education. *ASCD Education Update, 40*(7), 8.

Wolf, K. (1996). Developing an effective teaching portfolio. *Educational Leadership, 53*(6), 34-37.

Wong, H. (1998). *The first days of school.* Sunnyvale, CA: Author.

Index

**CORWIN
PRESS**

The Corwin Press logo—a raven striding across an open book—
represents the happy union of courage and learning. We are a
professional-level publisher of books and journals for K–12 educators,
and we are committed to creating and providing resources that em-
body these qualities. Corwin's motto is "Success for All Learners."